Perestroika Glasnost and Socialism

T0078281

Perestroika Glasnost and Socialism

K Vijayachandran

PARTRIDGE
A Penguin Random House Company

To order additional copies of this book, contact
Partridge India
000 800 10062 62
www.partridgepublishing.com/india
orders.india@partridgepublishing.com

CONTENTS

PREFACE

Einstein wrote his celebrated essay; **Why Socialism?,** in the inaugural issue of Monthly Review which reprinted it in 1998, to mark its golden jubilee.

The essay concluded with a couple of questions: The achievement of socialism requires the solution of some extremely difficult socio-political problems: how is it possible, in view of the far-reaching centralization of political and economic power, to prevent bureaucracy from becoming all-powerful and overweening? How can the rights of the individual be protected and therewith a democratic counterweight to the power of bureaucracy be assured?

Einstein was a great believer in the inevitability of socialism and his fears were legitimate. But did such an exigency, as feared by him, really develop in USSR, the first ever socialist state created by proletarian classes? Opening article of this book, written in 1989, examines this question, in detail, by analyzing the class roots, content and course of Perestroika and Glasnost movement of Gorbachev.

Lenin had theorized that imperialism was the highest order that capitalism could reach, and Bolshevik revolution had debated, in detail, the prospects of building socialism in one country. Liberation of a hundred nations and nationalities from Czarist oppression and creation of a multinational state based on the peaceful coexistence of diverse cultures was, possibly, the most significant historical achievement of Soviet revolution.

India as a multinational country has many things to learn from the Soviet experiment as well as the experience of CIS and the erstwhile CMEA countries. Articles on the development experience of India, reproduced in this book, highlight the unfinished tasks of national liberation in our multinational country, ruled by an anti-people coalition under the influence of global monopoly capital.

The twenty articles in this collection were written and published over a period of two decades: They are reproduced as they were, with minor editorial corrections: Title represents the true spirit behind the book project.

September 18, 2013
K Vijayachandran

REACTION STRIKES EUROPE

This eight part article was written in December 1989, about two years before the dismantling and final collapse of USSR. It was written at a time when the entire world was speculating on the prospects of Gorbachev's perestroika and glasnost. At that time, I was affiliated to CPI(M)—the Communist Party of India (Marxist), and the article was scheduled for publication in the Marxist, the theoretical quarterly of that party. For reasons unknown, the article was not published by Marxist or any other party journal. However, it was widely circulated within the top leadership of CPI(M) and served as a valuable input for inner party discussions on Soviet reforms. The document tries to interpret the reforms based on the class contradictions that had developed within the Soviet society over a period of seven decades.

I

"A spectre is haunting Europe; the spectre of Communism. All the Powers of old Europe have entered into a holy alliance to exorcise this specter: Pope and Czar, Metternich and Guizot, French Radicals and German police spies."— These were the opening words of the Manifesto of the

Communist Party, drawn up by a secret conclave of communists of a few European nationalities assembled in London in November 1847. The Manifesto concluded with the appeal: "The Communists disdain to conceal their views and aims. They openly declare that their ends can be attained only by the forcible overthrow of all existing social conditions. Let the ruling classes tremble at a Communistic revolution. The proletarians have nothing to loss but their chains. They have a world to win: WORKING MEN OF ALL COUNTRIES UNITE!"

A series of uprisings by proletariat swept Europe in 1848 and 1849 and within twenty-five years of the first printing of the Manifesto there was the Paris Commune of 1871 when World's first government of the dictatorship of the proletariat was established; but it lasted only seventy two days. Communists were hunted down; worker demonstrators were shot down as in Chicago on the 1st of May 1886 or arrested, imprisoned and tortured. Battles were fought at the plane of economic theories and political ideas; capitalists the world over ridiculed Marxism as shear nonsense or at the best as an utopia.

The numerous struggles and battles fought by the proletariat, through out the world, were not in vain. Seventy years after the Manifesto, the first proletarian state was born in 1917, toward the end of first world war, imposed over the mankind by the bourgeoisie classes, the capitalists all over the world tried all means, both foul and fair, in order to sabotage the first proletarian state including direct intervention. Soviet Union not only survived all such intrigues but also proved the dictatorship of the proletariat to be a viable alternative political system superior even to the bourgeoisie system.

Faced with the challenge thrown up by working class the bourgeois experimented with and encouraged fascist dictatorships as in Germany, Italy and Spain, throwing to winds their democratic pretensions. The ultimate result was a ruinous Second World War in which several millions perished. Socialism became an even more attractive proposition to more and more nations whose people liberated themselves from the oppressive capitalist system using Marxism as a creative tool. The socialist camp with about one third of humanity and the non-aligned group of third world countries, with more than half of world population, who had liberated themselves from the colonial yokes and with strong anti-imperialist sentiments were a direct challenge to the global ambitions of imperialist countries. Development of the socialist economies during the post war years, in spite of the cold war conditions imposed by imperialists, was commendable. Share of the socialist block in world industrial production which was hardly 20 per cent in 1950 increased to 40 percent by 1983. And, the share of developed capitalist economies came down drastically during the same period.

All the above are historical facts which even the capitalist ideologues may not dispute. Capitalist classes of the world were mortally afraid of the spread of Marxian ideology. In their jargon, of course, the increasing popularity of socialistic ideas was the result of Soviet or Chinese, expansionism. Containing communism was the official policy of all capitalist states, especially those of the developed capitalist countries. Totality of the war machine including the latest attempted star-war program of the Reagan Government, the troops stationed on far off foreign soils, the huge espionage and propaganda network, subversion of Governments of third world countries, imposition of dictators over the unwilling peoples, economic and development policies dictated through institutions like World Bank and the IMF and the numerous other programs and policies were all pursued by the developed capitalist Governments, under the leadership of the United States of America with the single-mindedness of containing communism. Peter Drucker known as the grand old guru of corporate capitalism in the Western World, while discussing the prospects of corporate business for the nineties in a recent article in the Economist had commented with satisfaction:

"The lodestar by which the free world has navigated since the late 1940s, the containment of Russia and of communism is becoming obsolescent, because of that policy's very success."(l).

Capitalist classes the world over; their theoreticians and propagandists see the recent developments in the socialist world as a great source of comfort and consolation. They feel that their efforts at containing of communism have at last succeeded after one and a half century and the specter that haunted Europe has been exorcised! They take legitimate pride in their success. Reaction has struck Europe and the working class movement all over the world is, at least for the moment, on the defensive. And this fact needs to be accepted with openness and candor.

II

Capitalists are at their best in marketing, not only of the goods they produce but also of ideas and ideologies. They know how best to utilize opportunities and reap maximum profits. There never were better times to market capitalist ideology. They sold tons and tons of the broken-down Berlin Wall in attractive packages at several hundred dollars a kilo. Every gram of that material, they count, will keep on reminding the people, generations after generations, of the brutal atrocities perpetrated by an inhuman and inefficient system called communism!

Edward Mortimer commentator of Financial Times London, speculating on the impact of the changes in the socialist countries on international relations of the nineties remarked: "Second half of this decade has seen a truly astonishing drama—the end of Communism as—we know—and perhaps even the end of "communism" as a name as any one will think worth using for a utopia that we know not yet . . . . Perhaps Russia would have progressed faster, economically and educationally if in 1917, had it adopted some other system; that we can never know for sure. Certainly few other *systems* could have exacted such a terrible price for what they did achieve. But this barbaric system was one that could be imposed on a backward, predominantly rural country, in conditions of international conflicts and then civil war. Even after 1945 the Soviet peoples were still helpless against it. But between 1945 and 1985 it did somehow produce a highly educated elite, comprising (it now seems) at least some millions of people, who took a minimum of civil and international peace for granted, and judged their own country by the highest international standards, not only of military technology but of civilization in the broader sense. They judged it, and found it wanting." **(2)**

Perhaps, it was superficial to quote a Western Commentator on the "failure of Communism". The views of a prominent member of the highly educated elite, referred to by Mortimer, Dr. Abalkin, Dy. Prime Minister of USSR and considered the economics guru of Gorbachev, could have served the purpose even better. He had been to Brussels recently for negotiating cooperation agreements with the European Community. In a press conference there he stated that 'there were 40 million Soviet citizens (15 per cent of the population) who find themselves in due economic straits after having worked for all their lives'. According to Western press reports "he all but claimed developing country status for the Soviet Union!" (3). The Soviet Union which considerably outstrips the USA in the production of oil, gas, steel, fertilizers, machine tools, tractors, harvesters, wheat, milk, butter and other diary products, fish, textiles, shoes and several other commodities; a country which has many more doctors, hospital beds, scientists and scientific institutions, teachers and educational institutions than the USA, a country which is a world leader in space and military technology, and considered a superpower till yesterday to match the combined military might of all developed capitalist countries taken together, claims today only the status of a developing country!

What has gone wrong with the Dy. Prime Minister of the Soviet Union who is supposed to be a communist and a member of the highly educated elite class as maybe certified by Western Commentators? Apart from denigrating the achievements of the Soviet people over the past seven decades, he was expounding his wisdom on the recent history of mankind as well, in that press conference at Brussels. While discussing on colonialism he told the reporters: "Soviet Union has long argued that the poverty of developing countries are the direct result of colonialism. The idea that the prosperity of colonial powers rested on their exploitation of the colonies is too simplistic a view of history. Rather it was due to West's organizational skills, especially as applied to production, a trained work force, respect for work and property and basically democratic values' (3)

And, Dr. Abalkin ridiculed the argument that economic development of the third world countries is a major responsibility of the former colonial powers: Even a hard core imperialist would not dare, today, to air such views in public! Even the commentator of Financial Times who admired him and the elite class of the Soviet Union had lamented on the existing economic relationship between the developed and developing countries: "In a grotesque inversion of all rational economics, the poorer two thirds of the World has steadily reduced its living standards in order to transfer resources to the richer one third. It is perhaps surprising that we in the North while shedding crocodile tears over this phenomenon from time to time have bothered less and less about the third World'. (2) That, precisely, is the situation prevailing in the so called integrated interdependent world of today, as seen even by a bourgeoisie propagandist. But Dr. Abalkin and his ilk have a totally different interpretation of history. These are the very people who are now trying to rewrite the history of Soviet Union on the pretext that what exists today is a grossly distorted version, fabricated by Stalinists!

A good many of such statements made by responsible Soviet leaders like Dr. Abalkin contradicts not only Marxian understanding of history but even the contemporary perceptions of capitalist world. The demands to do away with central planning in Soviet economy, to dismantle the large complex organizations that were built over a period of time, and to leave everything to the market mechanism and competition are typical examples. Theories on price formation under market mechanism have practically nothing to do with the ground realities and this is a widely accepted position today even among capitalist economists. Formation of large conglomerates, business groups and multinational corporations in the capitalist world, is not even a recent phenomenon and they operate under shared monopoly conditions. Even the much trumpeted experiments of Thatcher with large scale privatization in the name of promoting competition and vigor in the British economy have already lost their charm.

In the meanwhile global corporations of the capitalist world seems to be moving more and more away from market competition to what they call as strategic alliance: ' Kenichi Ohame, the author of 'The mind of the strategist', in his Harvard Business Review article on 'The global Logic of Strategic Alliance" argues that, in a changeable world of rapidly globalizing markets and industries, a world of converging consumer tastes, rapidly spreading technology, escalating fixed costs and growing protectionism, alliance is an essential tool for serving customers. According to him, globalization mandates alliance and makes them absolutely essential to strategy. According to Jet Magsaysay, the executive editor of World Executive's Digest, as the business environment, both locally and internationally, becomes increasingly competitive; companies will have more reason and will find more ways to form strategic alliances. As that happens, strategic alliances will not only be a logical alternative but a key to survival in business. Management experts predict that in the not-too-distant future, alliances will be a necessity not only for individual companies but also for orderly development of entire industries and those companies in mature, slow-growth industries will increasingly look to strategic alliances for survival." (4).

The Corporate business strategies likely to be followed by the West in the nineties are obvious from the above observations by the leading consultants of global corporations. The rapid development of cheap information processing and transmission capabilities thanks to the microelectronics revolution is being extensively made use of by corporate capitalism in order to simplify organizational methods and at the same time to strengthen their muscle power. To quote again Peter Drucker from his paper on corporate perspectives for the nineties: 'Business will undergo more, and more radical, restructuring in the 1990s than at any time since the modern corporate organization first evolved in the 1920s. Only five years ago it was treated as sensational news when I pointed out that the information-based organization needs far fewer levels of management than the traditional command and control model. By now a great many, may be most, large American companies have cut management levels by one-third or more. But the restructuring of corporations, middle-sized ones as well as large ones, and, eventually, even smaller ones; has barely begun." (1)

In fact at one point of time the Harvard Management experts were apprehensive that the Soviet Union's enormous planning and organizational experience, if coupled with the new information technology, will be a formidable threat for the capitalist World. But present day Soviet economists, who are in power, are more keen to dismember and dismantle the large public sector organizations, in order to overcome the difficulties with the unwieldy command structures, rather than seeking technological solutions which are feasible and being implemented by corporate capitalism.

How could the elite classes and the intelligentsia of the Soviet Union who pose themselves as radicals and progressives and commended upon by many Western political analysts as the only hope for that country be so backward in their economic theories, political thinking and views on history? One need not even question the relevance of glasnost and perestroika in the present situation but, the lack of seriousness with which reform proposals are put up and debated today raises genuine doubts about the quality of the present leadership of Soviet party and government.

While reporting on the three day conference in November at Moscow, where Dr.Abalkin presented his long term perspectives for the restructuring of Soviet economy, Quentin Peel another Financial Times analyst quoted the words of a Soviet factory worker: "We began to go wrong in the Soviet Union with Khrushchev, when we started to introduce elements of capitalism into communism. The two systems cannot mix. We must go back to the 1950s." (5) Peel's assessment was that these words reflected the gut reaction of many in the audience. More than 700 economists, 500 factory and farm managers and selected members of the public, according to the analyst more than 1400 of the best brains in the Soviet Union, participated in this conference. The corner stone of the proposed reforms was fundamental changes in property relations. The program was rightly commented on by the analyst as a program for social democracy, and according to him the tenor of the debate was "powerful pressure from the conservatives (i.e. anti-reformists)' Dr.Ed. Hewitt a leading US specialist on Soviet economy reportedly commented after the first day of the debate: "Western economists know how to manage a market economy. They do not know how to create it from the scratch. That is what they are trying to do here".

The claim that Western economists know how to manage a market economy may sound a little hollow, judging from the way they grapple with the never ending crisis in world capitalism. But Dr.Hewitt was outright honest when he stated that they will not be in a position to help Dr.Abalkin, and that his plans for building, in the Soviet Union, a market economy from the scratch were beyond their comprehension. The sophisticated reaction of this US expert is not much different in essence from the blunt words of the Soviet factory worker, "that capitalism and communism just cannot mix. But Dr.Abalkin who is described by Peel "as the first true member of the intelligentsia in the Government" as well as his colleagues have different views and they are pressurizing the Soviet people to accept their reform proposals. There are any numbers of reports indicating that reforms aimed at fundamental changes in property relationships are being resented by the vast majority of Soviet people, not necessarily through the mass media but on the ground, whenever such reforms are implemented piecemeal on an experimental basis. Reform enthusiasts blame the workers fir this, calling them lazy indifferent people, insensitive to the needs of society. The Supreme Soviet in its sitting in mid-December has, in the meanwhile, decided that the reforms on the lines of Dr.Abalkin's proposals will be implemented only after three years, starting from 1993, as the second stage of an overall reform package placed before it by the Prime Minister Ryzhkov.

III

How is that Dr.Abalkin, the true representative of the intelligentsia in Soviet Government is in a position to push on with such reform plans, judged as basically unsound even by Western experts, in spite of the widespread reservations and resentment expressed by the Soviet people? The assessment of the Soviet factory worker that, 'we began to go wrong in the Soviet Union with Khrushchev" provides once again a clue to the genesis and character of the present reform movement. Edward Mortimen the western commentator describes the rise in the role of the intelligentsia or the elite who is heading the perestroika movement in Soviet Union: "The elite gradually found its voice as the repression deployed to keep it in the line softened, from the extremes of barbarism under Stalin to the still disgusting but limited unpleasantness of Brezhnev. The foremost member and shining symbol of it was of course, Andrei Sakharov. A carrier like his would have been unthinkable in Stalin's time". (2)

Equating the rule of the dictatorship of the proletariat with barbarism is not a new interpretation from Western Commentators and it is as old as the October Revolution itself; there might have been excesses under Stalin not only against intellectuals but also against other human beings, typical of revolutionary situations. But to say that the intelligentsia could not find its voice due to Stalinist repression, no doubt is a gross exaggeration. Does it not imply that Stalin and the working class party built up a Soviet State to the status of a super power, single handed and without the help of the intelligentsia?

The truth is that the finest among the intelligentsia and the vast majority of the scientists, engineers, economists and planners, inspired by the visions of a new society cooperated with Stalin and the working class party to build up the first proletarian State under the most hostile circumstances of conspiracies and sabotages organized by world capitalism.

It is true that a small minority of egoistic intellectuals represented by Trotsky and others were not permitted to dominate the party. Their views and alternatives regarding building up a new socialist economy were debated for several years within the party and ultimately rejected by the working class. These are all part of recorded history.

But the situation began to change since Khrushchev's reforms when the CPSU started transforming itself from a working class party to a party of the whole people. Material incentives were given undue importance and radical changes were introduced in the management of economy. True, the problems of managing and coordinating a rapidly diversifying Soviet economy was getting more and more complex. Discussing on the management problems of the Soviet economy Brezhnev had stated in his report to the 26th Congress of the CPSU in 1981: "Different variants and different schemes, as you know have been tried out. A great deal of diversified experience has been accumulated. The experience makes it clear that the quest, it seems, is towards greater independence of the amalgamations and enterprises and greater powers and responsibility of economic managers".

Granting greater and greater independence and autonomy for the enterprises without the matching information feed back to central planning authorities was sure recipe for undermining the planning process. Enterprises and their managers were becoming more and more autonomous but less and less accountable. Economic managers were growing more and more powerful and independent, many of them becoming corrupt, some even millionaires and capable of buying up trade union and party functionaries. Checks and balances provided by working class democracy through the primary party bodies were getting weakened. Brezhnev lamented in his report to 26th Congress: "Primary Party organizations are vested with the right to control the work of managements. It is important that they exercise this right to a larger extent and in the best way possible. Whether it is a matter of personnel, the fulfillment of economic plans, or the improvement of people's working and living conditions, the Party organizations should adopt a principled stand and not take their cue from the management when the latter is wrong. In short, they should firmly implement the Party line."

A careful reading of the reports to successive congresses of CPSU by its general Secretaries will reveal this increasing weakness of the party organization at various levels to assert itself on questions of economic management. This has in turn led to the rule of bureaucrats and managers. A situation where economic enterprises were managed more like capitalist enterprises, offering material incentives to the workers with very little participation or control by the organized working class and the trade unions was emerging gradually but steadily.

Gorbachev in his report to the 27th Congress had stated: "In our country, the trade unions are the largest mass organization. On the whole, they do a lot to satisfy the requirements of factory and office workers and collective farmers, to promote emulation, tighten discipline and heighten labor productivity. Still trade union committees are in many cases lacking in militancy and resolve when it comes to defending the working people's legitimate interests, ensuing labor protection and safety, and constructing and running health-building, sports and cultural facilities. Understandably such passivity suits those managers for whom production sometimes obscures the people. The trade unions, however, should always give priority to social policy objectives, to promoting the working people's interests. Properly speaking, this is the basic purpose of their activity. The all union Central Council of Trade Unions and other trade union bodies enjoy extensive rights and control considerable funds, both the state's and their own. It is up to them, therefore, to make extensive and confident use of them, instead of waiting for somebody else to fulfill the tasks they are charged with"

In order to strengthen the party and to enable it to play the due leadership role more effectively several steps were being taken. The decisions taken in this direction by the 25th Congress as well as the outcome of their implementation were reported by Brezhnev in his report to the 26th Congress: "In accordance with the instructions of the 25th Congress, many specialists working in the economy were assigned to party work. At present three out of every four secretaries of the Central Committees of the Communist Parties of the Union republics and of territorial and regional committees and two out of every three secretaries of city and district Party Committees have a technical, economic or agricultural education. This is gratifying. But it must be taken into account that a segment of the specialists who have come into the Party apparatus from industry do not have sufficient political experience and in some cases, bring economic management methods into Party organs."

Brezhnev further criticized the lack of political training and experience of the comrades "appointed to party executive" work and emphasized the "need for their seasoning in the thick of working masses". It is not possible to ascertain how and to what extent politicalisation and ideological training of the experts and managers assigned to party leading bodies as is visualized by Brezhnev in 1981 could be accomplished. In Gorbachev's report to the next Congress in 1986 there is no specific mention in this regard. However he had more or less indicated the persistence of this shortcoming in the functioning of the party, as well as the Government.

Whether the specialists in the economy who were assigned to party work at the leading bodies of the party have adequate political and ideological background or not is no doubt a very important question. But the fact to be noted here is that the specialists and managers were being given a free hand in running economic enterprises in the name of autonomy and efficiency and at the same time they were being increasingly assigned key positions in the party, It is one thing to respect intellectuals and their knowledge and to provide them with the best of living conditions but, it is another thing to permit their hegemony over the party.

It was erroneous to believe that class contradictions had ceased to exist in the Soviet society and that the specialists and managers will not have their own class interests. The specialists, the managers and the academics or the intelligentsia as they are referred to generally in the Soviet Union have their common views and perceptions about life which are conditioned by objective realities, both internal and external to Soviet Society. They have their group interests and group aspirations which were sure to assert themselves on the society and the party as sectarian class interests, unless contained politically and ideologically. This basic Marxian understanding was overlooked when Khrushchev's reforms gradually changed the CPSU from a working class party to a party of the whole Soviet people'.

Members of professional classes or the intelligentsia have been joining the CPSU in larger numbers; party members having post graduate or doctoral degrees increased by 14 times during the period 1950 to 1983. Brezhnev in his report to the 26th Congress had noted with some satisfaction: "the influx of Soviet intelligentsia to the party continued during the reporting period". The quota system for membership was abolished recently and reports for the period 1986—88 indicate that more and more members of the intelligentsia have been joining the party ever since the current reforms started. However more than the absolute or relative strength of the intelligentsia in terms of numbers it is the preeminent position they have come to enjoy not only in the economic life but also in the political life of Soviet Union which has made the qualitative difference since Khrushchev's reforms.

IV

It is necessary to understand the perceptions, the aspirations and the social background of the intelligentsia as a class in order to appraise their role in present day Soviet society. They are the elite, the better educated and the chief custodians of knowledge and expertise generated over the years by Soviet Society. Under socialism, all assets, tangible or intangible, material or intellectual, created through the process of social production stand transferred to the society. But the perception of intelligentsia is that the wealth of expertise they possess were partly inherited and partly acquired by them in their individual, capacity. They consider these as their personal property. Under capitalist relations of production owner of any property physical or intellectual (the latter is getting more and more importance today in the capitalist world) are entitled for rent or royalty, which in essence means profits or a claim for a larger share in social production. There are no upper limits for incomes from property under capitalism but wage incomes are restricted through the mechanism of labor market and a minimum of unemployment. Unlike under socialism, where growth and development are based on social consensus, income differentials in favor of property owners are the motive force for economic growth under capitalism; higher the differential higher is the propensity for growth.

Intelligentsia of Soviet Union who consider themselves as the owners of substantial intellectual property look at their counterparts in capitalist world—the corporate managers of industry and commerce or the top bureaucrats in Government and draw up comparisons that are quite unpleasant for themselves. Their counterparts in corporate capitalism possess vast expensive villas, frequent the most expensive of clubs, pick up choicest luxuries from exclusive shops, enjoy holidays on the best of beaches with the very best of company, have all the freedom, the freedom of the modern jet-set, and above all the freedom for lording over their fellow citizens with the right to 'hire and fire'. After enjoying all the wonderful hospitalities offered by his counterparts in a capitalist country during a brief visit there, a Soviet manager as he returns home, looks at his own country as extremely backward, uncivilized and even barbarian and considers himself a "prisoner of working class democracy!"

Russian intelligentsia at the time of the October Revolution was a mixed lot. A small minority had allied itself with the working class, in overthrowing the autocracy of Czar. After the revolution, a large number immigrated to capitalist countries, declaring Bolshevism as a barbarian political ideology. Possibly a sizable minority stayed with the Bolsheviks, inspired by patriotism and idealism. But even they had a tough time in reconciling with the rigors of proletarian dictatorship. But it must be said to the credit of the Bolshevik party that the finest elements among the intelligentsia could be won over to the side of the revolution and they cooperated with the working class not only in building up the first socialist state, practically out of nowhere but also in the upbringing of a new generation of brain workers from the ranks of the working class. The Second World War generated intense patriotic sentiments, which continued unabated during the early periods of the cold war as well.

The absence of fear for tomorrow and the extensive of social security provided by the socialist system had created the best of conditions for the blooming of a creative intelligentsia in the Soviet Union. In fact Soviet society produced many more outstanding scientists, engineers, economists, artists and athletes than any of the capitalist countries including the USA. But international capitalism could offer them much higher prices than Soviet socialism. A few decades were long enough for the Soviet intelligentsia to distance itself from the idealism and patriotism of the proletarian revolution. Its perceptions and aspirations underwent a sea change; it began to see world capitalism as its natural ally and full of opportunities. In the name of democratization and de-Stalinization the concepts of proletarian internationalism and proletarian dictatorship were abandoned. Independent political initiative of the working class which was the main-stay of the power structure in the Soviet Union got weakened by the over-emphasis on material incentives and autonomy for the economic managers. We have seen that even the management of the CPSU was being taken over by specialists and academics at various levels. Top leadership of the party being surrounded by the elite classes was getting more and more isolated from the working class and the people but, continued to exercise its power and authority drawing heavily on the capital of past glory and prestige of a revolutionary party.

Economic managers who were positioned as party functionaries paid obeisance to the top leadership and the political power structure started assuming a feudal character. No more was it necessary for them to win over the hearts and minds of the working people and democracy was the worst casualty. Brezhnev's period was characterized as 'the period of stagnation' and by the time of 27th Congress the working class and the entire people were convinced that changes were inevitable.

V

Glasnost and Perestroika in their essence had meant correcting the earlier deviations by ensuring the broadest possible participation of the working people in the management of society. Documents of the 27th Congress as well as other official documents of the party regarding reforms had visualized the re-invigoration of the class and mass organizations as well as the primary party organizations on Leninist principles as the practical program for the deepening of democracy and for helping Perestroika. It was visualized that the initiative for the reforms will be taken by the party and implemented with the help of trade unions and other public organizations. But this did not happen. The experience of two years of reform movement is summarized by Onikov, a CPSU central committee official, in an interview: (6)

"Democratization has brought all strata of Soviet society into motion, creating an atmosphere of activity, innovation and a drive for eliminating shortcomings. In the absence of democratic traditions and relevant experience these unquestionably sound manifestations of democracy have been spontaneous and unorganized. Far from all party organizations and Communists have been prepared to head and encourage this social breakthrough. When unsound tendencies appear, party members do not always notice them in time and cannot counter and neutralize them.

This was alarmingly in evidence during events we are not accustomed to: meetings, strikes, riots, or demonstrations in different regions of the country.

Rank and file Communists could not decide how to react to them. They remained passive as usual, waiting for instructions from above."

Party apparatus was naturally handicapped to lead the reforms because the intelligentsia who were on the vanguard of the reform movement were also dominating the party leadership at various levels. They were already alienated from the masses as well as rank and file party workers and naturally they could not inspire the working class and their organizations. But the members of the intelligentsia who were holding leading positions within the party and the Soviet economy could easily rally themselves together and enlist the support of the non-party intellectuals and the anti-party elements in Soviet society, who were seeing the reforms as an opportunity to work towards their sectarian objectives. An informal pressure group led by the intelligentsia calling themselves 'radicals', having powerful influence over the party and the Government came into existence. The initiative for the reforms fell into the hands of this pressure group and every single reform measures suggested and discussed today in the Soviet Union are centered on the sectarian interests of the intelligentsia, who considers itself as the natural leaders of the Soviet society and the owners of its intellectual property.

The first and foremost step of this group was to hijack the media and use it extensively for ideological subversion about which Gorbachev himself had given a clear warning in his report to the 27th Congress: " The insidiousness and unscrupulousness of bourgeois propagandists must be countered with a high standard of professionalism on the part of our ideological workers, by the morality and culture of socialist society, by the openness of information, and by the incisive and creative character of our propaganda. We must be on the offensive in exposing ideological subversion and in bringing home truthful information about the actual achievements of socialism about the socialist way of life."

In their antisocialist and anti-Soviet propaganda, making full use the extensive Soviet mass media, the radicals have even outdone their counterparts in the imperialist world and the indications are that the Soviet people are fed up with this today. But, what is strange is that the perpetrators of this slanderous propaganda continue to hold key positions in Soviet party and Soviet Government in spite of the resentment expressed by the vast majority of Soviet people.

The radicals pose themselves as the champions of truth and democracy. But they have no qualms about spreading falsehood and even scandals. According to them, Stalin was the worst of all dictators, and in his time inner party democracy was unheard of. Brezhnev's period is characterized only as 'the period of stagnation'. The fact that democracy was at its worst during Brezhnev's time and at its best during Stalin's time when working class democracy was the guiding principle is often pushed under the carpet by the radicals but, is evident from an unintentional testimony by Onikov (6):

"During the long period of stagnation, especially in its last years, its democratic value was reduced to naught, and turned into a hollow formality, the like of which was not even seen in Stalin's time. By way of illustration let us take such a strong party organization as that of Moscow. up to 1940 there was not a single case at dozens of its conferences of a nominee for full or candidate membership of the regional or city party committee or the being elected unanimously. It was a common practice then, especially in the 1920s, that some of the candidates proposed were not elected. The first case when all candidates for full and candidate membership of the regional committee and the auditing commission were elected unanimously were recorded in 1974. Not a single candidate on the voting list was voted down in 1976 the same happened at the city party conference."

It is necessary to remember that during Brezhnev's time especially in his later years the specialists, the managers and the academics were holding the key positions in the party. Democracy and freedom professed by the radicals and practiced in the reform movement, today, in the Soviet Union are meant only for the intelligentsia, "the owners of intellectual property" and not for the working masses. This is even more evident from the proposals for economic reform drafted by Dr. Abalkin, referred to earlier. The corner stone of the reforms is changes in the property relations; or the freedom for different forms of property; public, cooperative and private to compete among themselves. When asked about the participation of the working people in the management of the economy Dr. Abalkin had reacted: (3).

"the toiling masses must be full masters of political and social life. The government's task was to restore socialist content, give to all toilers a say in running the country. This was not a near term prospect but the final goal of perestroika".

All talks of deepening of democracy on Leninist lines and such sentiments expressed in the revised party program of 1986 sound hollow in the context of the reform proposals put up by the Dy. Prime Minister of Soviet Union. The proposals visualize the creation of a labor market in socialist Soviet Union, denationalization of property and intensive development of foreign economic ties. It is clear that when hundreds of thousands of hectares of farm land are leased out to individuals or private enterprises, or public enterprises are handed over to Joint stock companies, or when new enterprises are set up with imperialist collaboration, it will be the members of the intelligentsia who will be managing them in the capacity of corporate managers or owning them, in the capacity of shareholders. In other words the Soviet Intelligentsia which consider themselves as the owners of intellectual property sees the current reforms as an opportunity for further tightening their strangle hold on the economy as a class, with the help as necessary from their foreign counterparts, the corporate managers of world capitalism. Their sectarian interests even compel them to shed all pretensions of patriotism, to depict the mighty Soviet Union as a 'developing country' and to play a subservient role to foreign monopoly capital and imperialism.

The blue print put up by the intelligentsia for the dismantling of the socialist system in Soviet Union has aggravated the nationality question within the Soviet Union. Though the Soviet intelligentsia across the nationalities is united, today, against the broad interests of the Soviet people, they are divided on ethnic lines. Disruption of ethnic harmony had started surfacing ever since the intelligentsia got an upper hand in the economic and political life of Soviet Union. Disruptive tendencies were somewhat dormant even in 1986 when Gorbachev assessed the situation in his report to the 27th Congress: "National oppression and inequality of all types and forms have been done away with once and for all. The indissoluble friendship among nations and respect for national cultures and for the dignity of all peoples has been established, and has taken firm root in the minds of tens of millions of people. The Soviet people are a qualitatively new social and international community, cemented by the same economic interests, ideology and political goals".

He warned about certain tendencies that have come up in recent times and emphasized the need to follow Lenin's teachings: "Our Party's tradition, traceable to Lenin of being particularly circumspect and tactful in all that concerns the nationalities policy and the interests of every nation or nationality, national feelings, calls at the same time for resolute struggle against national narrow mindedness and arrogance, nationalism and chauvinism, no matter what their guise may be".

But the Perestroika as it unpackaged itself, intensely aggravated the nationality problem. The fears of the peoples of the small nationalities and ethnic minorities about the re-emergence of 'Russian imperial domination were quite genuine in the context of reform proposals of the Abalkin type, and they rallied themselves behind the intelligentsia of the corresponding nationalities. The Soviet intelligentsia who had coined the concept of an 'integrated interdependent world' in order to morally justify their collaboration with the corporate managers of world capitalism find itself divided, today, on ethnic lines. When the capitalists of various nationalities of Western Europe, after prolonged squabbles and infighting among themselves, are succeeding in the creation of an integrated European Market the reform program of the Soviet intelligentsia is rapidly fragmenting the economy of Soviet Union.

The sectarian interests of the intelligentsia dominate every detail of the ideological package shaped up by the reformists or the radicals who are dishonest to the core. Their way of functioning is totally undemocratic as alleged by several of their own followers, their words and actions do not go together and every one of their theoretical formulations are aimed at politically browbeating the Soviet working class. They talk endlessly on Science and Technology and eulogize on the Scientific-Technological Revolution as if it is a post-Marxian phenomenon (meaning only we, the experts know it; you proletarians do not!). They endlessly sermonize on the fragile nature of environmental and ecological balance of the biosphere (you fools' you are sure to break it and destroy it!) on the integrated interdependent world (ignorant proletarians, do not meddle with it!), and on the invincibility of an impersonal, omnipotent and mystical market mechanism (only we experts can manage it and not your politics!). When they talk about freedom and human rights they are only asserting their own right to get a better price in the international market for the intellectual property or special skills they have come to possess while working for the Soviet society. They try to convince the people of Soviet Union that everything has gone wrong during past seven decades because of the politics of the working class and the early years of proletarian dictatorship. They try to depict Stalin as a barbarian and to resurrect Trotsky, whose perspectives for developing Soviet society were in tune with the sectarian aspirations of the intelligentsia of that period. Through every single instances of their words and deeds the 'radicals' betray their sectarian ambitions for establishing their hegemony over the working class of the Soviet Union.

VI

Developments in the East European Socialist countries are, as in the past years, more or less in step with those in the Soviet Union, the first Socialist State. These small socialist states, the products of the Second World War, had set up their own economic and political systems after the Soviet Model. However, the possibility of ideology of an international working class movement being used as a cover for 'Great Russian domination' over the small socialist states was a widespread apprehension among the peoples of the newly formed socialist countries of Europe. Such fears were, in fact, continuously reinforced by constant imperialist propaganda. The earlier Hungarian and Polish resistance against socialist governments as well as the Yugoslavian defiance of Stalin was rooted on the fear of such "Russian domination". The newly liberated countries and the national liberation movements of the non-European continents, especially those led by the working class as in China, Korea, Vietnam and Cuba had no such apprehensions and they had seen Soviet Union as a natural ally in their struggle against imperialism.

The economic and military alliance forged by the imperialist countries to contain communism and the so-called Russian expansionism was checkmated by a similar alliance of the European socialist countries led by the Soviet Union. The nonaligned movement of the third world countries was emerging itself as a third force championing the cause of a new world order with strong anti-imperialist sentiments and enjoying the sympathy and support of the socialist alliance. This was the international scenario that unfolded itself towards the final years of Stalin.

The reforms of Khrushchev had initiated a series of changes not only within the Soviet Union, as we have seen earlier, but also in international politics. Revisionist reform of Khrushchev could not get immediate acceptance within Soviet Union because of its long traditions of working class democracy: It suffered serious setbacks and ended up with the removal of Khrushchev himself from power. But the East European Socialist countries were a far more fertile soil for Khrushchev type reforms. Every one of these reforms, with the possible exemption of Albania, started rapidly traveling down the road of the new economic reforms. By 1967, the intelligentsia of Czechoslovakia had already hijacked the working class party and Government in that country and was about to establish their political hegemony over the people. Working class in that country which was supported by the new leadership of Soviet Union could reassert its leadership role once again in that country, at least temporarily.

Despite the change in leadership and removal of Khrushchev, the concept of transforming CPSIJ into a party of the whole people was getting concretized rapidly and as we have already seen, the hold of the intelligentsia over the economic enterprises, the administration and the party was getting more and more strengthened at the expense of working class democracy. The Soviet reform experiments were copied in other socialist countries as well, in varying degrees with the exception of, possibly, Cuba, Vietnam and Korea who were facing direct threats from imperialism. Even the international role of the Soviet Union was being perceived by the party leadership, dominated by the intelligentsia, more as that of a super power of paternal in character, which was distinctly different from the Stalinist traditions of equality and fraternity among nationalities. Thus the reform movement which started in the first socialist country spread to other countries as well, and ultimately led to the disruption of the international working class movement. Under the growing influence of the intelligentsia in party organization and leadership, communist parties all over the world with few exceptions started loosing their international perspectives: Euro-communism was a conspicuous example of this trend.

The revolt against the intelligentsia in China in the early sixties, the reassertion of working class democracy which took the form of the "cultural revolution", the withdrawal of Soviet technical assistance, the charges of social imperialism against Soviet Union and the eventual degeneration of the cultural revolution in to collaboration with the imperialists were all tremors that were triggered by the reform movement in Soviet Union, the first socialist state. The intelligentsia in the party succeeded once again to recapture its leading role in China and to strengthen itself as a class by making use of the economic reforms of the eighties and by exploiting the strong nationalist feelings of Chinese people. But its recent attempts to gain total hegemony over the Chinese people with the help of imperialism were halted at least temporarily. In Poland as a result of the reformist policies the Communist Party got itself completely isolated from the people and almost the entire working class crossed over to the Solidarity. In Hungary the working class party transformed itself into a bourgeois party, changed not only its name but also that of the republic. One of the first measures adopted by the new Government in Hungary was to ban political activity on the shop floor of the enterprises, and now a new working class party is being organized by the Hungarian Communists. In Czechoslovakia, in Bulgaria and in East Germany with the intelligentsia occupying key positions in politics as well as administration, hijacking of the Communist Party leadership was an extremely simple affair. After capturing the mass media a few massive demonstrations were organized and the party leaderships in these countries changed hands without a whimper.

The working class who lost their organizations overnight was forced to be a mere onlooker when rapid changes were taking place in these countries. There was of course stiff resistance in Rumania but the dissenters had the support of not only the imperialist camp but also of the Soviet Union as well as other socialist neighbors, whose governments had by then changed their class character. The remnants of working class democracy still existing in spite of several years of reformist movement in the East European socialist countries was overcome with ease, at least temporarily, by the joint efforts; of the corporate managers of socialism in these countries and the Soviet Union with the active support of the imperialist powers. The increasing resistance from the working class in Soviet Union would have prompted the 'radicals' of that country to intervene in the East European countries with out delay and to pull down the existing governments there. This was necessary for the radicals of the Soviet Union in order to consolidate their shaky position in their own country.

VII

Bourgeoisie ideologues sum up the emerging international situation with obvious satisfaction: 'corporate socialism' and "corporate capitalism have confluenced to the pursuit of a 'Common European Home' and the specter of communism and class struggle were exorcised from Europe. "End of history"—that was how Francis Fukuyama, the deputy director of U.S. departments policy staff, titled his thesis on the developments in socialist countries. In his view Marxian interpretation of history in terms of class struggles and conflicts, has become irrelevant and the present epoch represents the ultimate, the inevitable and irreversible victory of liberal capitalism over all other political ideologies including fascism and communism. According to him man's ideological evolution has come to an end and hereafter, it will be only an endless pursuit of technology. Fukuyama's thesis published in last summer and sold out in matter of minutes had prophesied: "The passing of Marxism—Leninism first from China and then from the Soviet Union will mean its death as a living ideology of world historical significance. For while there may be some isolated true believers left in places like Managua, Pyongyang, or Cambridge, Massachusetts, the fact that there is not a single large state in which it is a going concern undermines completely its pretensions to being in the vanguard of human history."

However just a few weeks after the Fukuyama's prophesy came in print, events in China unfolded themselves in a totally unexpected manner. In spite of the massive propaganda buildup and active support from imperialist agencies for subversion, China's political system survived. All sorts of postures from the high pedestals of morality and principles as well as economic sanctions were resorted to in order to pressurize Socialist China. But, on September 29th, celebrating the 40th Anniversary of the Chinese revolution Jiang Zemin the new General Secretary of Chinese Communist party declared on unequivocal terms: ' Victory in this struggle has further proved that the Chinese people's choice of the socialist road and the cause of socialist reform being carried out by them under the Leadership of the Chinese Communist Party have become the irreversible tide of history over the entire vast territory of China. No difficulties can stop, and no internal and external hostile forces can shake or alter, the advance and development of socialist China."

The administration of USA had to send its former President Nixon to patch up with the Chinese people; all other imperialist countries had to follow the US example one by one. Fukuyema along with many other bourgeoisie ideologues' dreams that with the death of Marxian ideology and the collapse of the socialist system, all the resistance against 'common marketization of the world' under the hegemony of the corporate managers of world capitalism could be easily overcome'. Of course they are not idle dreamers, Peter Drucker sums up the business strategy of the nineties for the global managers:(l): "Business tomorrow will follow two new rules, One: to move work to where the people are, rather than people to where the work is. Two: to farm out activities that does not offer opportunities for advancements into fairly senior management and professional positions (e.g. clerical work, maintenance, the 'Back office' in the brokerage house, the drafting room in the large architectural firm, the medical lab in the hospital) to an outside contractor. The corporation, in stock market jargon, will be unbundled."

Unbundling of the activities of global corporations and subcontracting out across the globe and thereby maneuvering the global labor market in order to reduce labor costs will thus be a major strategy to be followed by corporate capitalism. Realignment among the global corporations through strategic alliances and avoiding competition in order to optimize profits and to ensure a proper mix of long term and short term profits are the other components, as we have seen earlier, of the broad business strategy to be followed by corporate capitalism during the nineties. Peter Drucker, quoting the findings of Prof. Michael C. Johnson of Harvard University, states that "large business houses, especially in the USA are rapidly going private' and sum up the trend: "They (the global corporations) are putting themselves under the control of a small number of large share holders; and in such a way that their holders' self interest lies in building "long-term value rather than reaping immediate stock exchange gains."

All, these years the apologists of capitalism have been finding fault with Marx for his failure to see the possibility of democratic capitalism; that is corporate capitalism with extensively distributed shareholdings among the public, including workers. Corporate theoreticians are singing a different tune, now: "In order to ensure long term benefits for the society and to reduce costs, a global production system should be perfected with the help of strategic alliances of global corporations which should be owned and managed by a tiny but highly responsible group of shareholders and corporate managers!"

Whatever be the social benefits predicted by these theoreticians under the new dispensation, it is proof for the inevitability under capitalism of a small minority coming to own and control the means of production at a global level as predicted by Marx. Even when historical developments are vindicating Marx, bourgeoisie ideologues keep shouting from the housetops on the premature death of Marxism!

It is and it has been, all these years, a habit with bourgeoisie ideologues to declare Marxism as irrelevant and outdated. When the corporate managers of world capitalism are giving finishing touches to a global production system under their hegemony towards the end of the twentieth century their denunciation of Marxism of the nineteenth century as old and outdated may very well look justified. But some 150 years ago, the Communist Manifesto had observed: "The bourgeoisie, by the rapid improvement of all instruments of production, by the immensely facilitated means of communication draws all, even the most barbarian nations to civilization. The cheap prices of its commodities are the heavy artillery with which it batters down all Chinese walls, with which it forces the barbarians' intensely obstinate hatred of foreigners to capitulate. It compels all nations, on pain of extinction; to adopt the bourgeois mode of productions it compels them to introduce what it calls civilization into their midst, i.e to become bourgeois themselves. In one word, it creates a world after its own image1'.

A global production system under the hegemony of capitalists as visualized by Marx and Engeles had not come into vogue in 1827, when they drafted the Communist Manifesto. Even the bourgeois of Europe who were indulging in wars and destruction could not even imagine that they were slowly but steadily working toward perfecting of a global production machine of massive proportions. In those days it was only a tendency which Marx and Engels took notice of and made their brilliant prediction of an emerging global bourgeoisie and as its antithesis an international working class.

The dreams of a global production system and highly diversified commodity and labor market at the global level but, integrated under the hegemony of a tiny group of shareholders and corporate managers in the developed capitalist countries are now slowly emerging toward the end of the twentieth century. According to the visions of the bourgeoisie the millions over millions of proletarians of different trades and vocations and of different nationalities who will be a mere appendage of the global production system will, be politically and spiritually satisfied with the magic band of "social democracy" controlled by a tiny minority of global property owners and operated through the mechanism of market, public legislation and routine administration of justice. Mortimer the Financial Times Analyst models up the attitude of the modern proletariat to such a global system in the backdrop of Soviet experience (2): "Communism was an attempt at an historical short cut, adopted by relatively small groups of intellectuals and class-conscious workers in countries in the early stages of industrialization. A fully-formed industrial working class tends to prefer some form of social democracy, while the atomized 'Post-Fordist' workers of today when strictly industrial jobs require a high level of education and relatively unskilled jobs are to be found mainly in the service sector; may turnout not to be interested in socialism of any sort."

In effect an Orwellian model of society wherein a small minority equipped with an all powerful modern mass media forces down its political hegemony over the "proles' who are not concerned about politics is the bourgeois vision for the future of mankind. A sizeable minority among the managers, the academics and the intelligentsia in Soviet Union and other European Socialist countries may have their own dreams about playing an equal, but more likely a subsidiary role, in the global production system now visualized by the corporate managers of world capitalism. But how far the working class of these countries, especially that of the Soviet Union, with its long traditions of proletarian democracy, will be prepared to compromise their freedom and political privileges for the sake of 'Social. Democracy' is something that history will reveal itself. But as we have seen earlier, indications are that there is strong resistance in Soviet Union from the working class against the content and the direction that Perestroika has assumed under the leadership of the radicals.

A recent opinion survey conducted by a Soviet Sociological Research Institute revealed that the vast majority of Muscovites, who had given Yeltsin a massive mandate to the Supreme Soviet were opposed to the interpretations given by the radicals to Perestroika. They were against changes in property relations and large income inequalities, for social equity and justice, for strengthening of the socialist system within Soviet Union and for strengthening the economic ties with in the socialist world. The authors of this study, which was published in the Soviet periodical 'Twentieth Century and Peace' after seeing that hardly * 17 per cent of the Muscovites had supported their interpretation of Perestroika had lamented; ' After all how many for genuine perestroika?". The situation is rapidly changing in the Soviet Union and the working class has started asserting itself in order to defend the gains of socialism; even the attitudes and perceptions of the intelligentsia are slowly changing as was evident from the recent conference which discussed Dr.Abalkin's proposals for economic reforms.

The reform movement which started long back in Poland and Hungary after having failed to bring in major structural changes in the economy is now trying to take satisfaction by changing the name of republic or the party. Injecting "elements of capitalism into socialism" is proving itself to be an uphill task and also a messy one. It appears that the confusion and chaos created by the reforms could be resolved only by parceling out vast segments of their national economies and their taking over by foreign capitalist corporations. The possibility of such maneuvers and their success will be decided by the attitude and mood of the working class in these countries which though somewhat indifferent today under the conditions of ideological confusion created by the bourgeoisie and lack of organization, should not be taken for granted.

It is to be noted that even the attitude and perceptions of the working class in the imperialist countries under "social democracy" are rapidly changing today. Apart from the problems of persistent unemployment and deteriorating social welfare schemes, new types of threats and tensions are being created as the corporate managers of world capitalism are giving finishing touches to the global production system. Their plans for strategic alliances among global corporations are naturally aimed at the proletariats of different countries who could be easily browbeaten and played against each other by the global managers through the clever manipulations of a global labor market. Business activities of a global corporation could be 'unbundled' and palmed out to be sub-contracted across national boundaries to its own subsidiaries or to other global corporations in order to overcome labor resistance in a particular country or region.

A fragmented proletariat or "the atomized Post-Fordist workers" as referred to by the consultants of global business are proving to be more and more powerless today in the hands of a few corporate managers armed with an all powerful global information system. The possibilities for instant closures or retrenchments as well as instant switching of production activities across the globe to any or several locations without loss of business and profits are becoming a near term possibility with the rapid progress in data processing capabilities and expansion of global communication system. The global managers of USA are already resorting to such maneuvers in order to browbeat the American trade unions. The Vice President of the AFLCIO reacted with bitterness: "These Sons of the bitches" has to be taught a lesson through solidarity action by the international working class. The trade unions of USA as well as other imperialist countries are becoming increasingly conscious about the need for the international unity of working class.

VIII

Capitalist system can sustain itself and survive only if it keeps on expanding; stagnation means crisis and collapse. The world as we live have its limits, but because of its inner contradictions capitalism is not able to reach anywhere near these limits. The only incentive for expansion of capitalist system is private profit or personal greed. The rich getting richer and poor getting poorer need not be in absolute terms but certainly in relative terms is an absolute law that governs capitalism.

The imperialist countries of today or the 'North' as they call themselves were the early starters on the capitalist path. The rich in the North has by now become fabulously rich and the working people there enjoy far better living conditions compared to their counterparts in the South i.e. the developing countries. The gap between the North and the South keep on widening day after day and this will be so, so long as relations between the two continue on capitalist lines. The North keeps on pushing the South into a deeper and deeper debt trap.

The North just cannot accept the South on equal terms. It means redeeming the South of its massive debts and the wealth amassed by the rich of the North. That is an instant recipe for crisis and collapse of the system. The south on its own cannot accept unequal terms. But the ruling classes of the South have compromised themselves to be junior partners of the rich monopolists of the North but, the revolt of its people is gaining strength day after day.

The imperialists would like to bulldoze their way and they had been doing it but, the socialist camp was a deterrent all these years. With or without the support of the socialist camp the South will rally themselves around and resist such moves, the recent response to the Panama incident is only an indicator. Even if the North succeeds in bulldozing, that is no solution to the crisis in capitalism because it means getting back to the centuries old colonial regimes. North cannot extricate and isolate itself from the South because that will mean foregoing its claims on the debtors, crisis and collapse of the capitalist system, and tacit transition to planned economy, socialism or communism. That also means demise of the capitalist system even before it has reached the limits of the world that we live in.

There is no solution under the framework of capitalism for the problems faced by the 'integrated interdependent world' of today. Capitalism cannot further expand and come out of its crisis by continuing on the path of extensive growth as seen by the nineteenth and twentieth centuries. Its days are numbered; the bourgeois and the global managers of corporate capitalism are on their last wicket.

Extensive growth of capitalism not being possible any more and blocked by the North-South polarization of the world, the bourgeoisie is now fine-tuning the global production machine under its hegemony for intensifying exploitation in order to avoid a crisis and collapse of the system. Smaller and smaller groups of shareholders owning bigger and bigger global corporations and strategic alliances among them in order to maneuver the international labor market are, as we have seen, the grand strategies now being finalized by the global managers of corporate capitalism. All such maneuvers by the rich in the North are intended for the intensive exploitation of the working class of the North and then the South as a whole but will help the imperialists and the monopolists only to delay their ultimate downfall.

The working class and the trade unions of USA and other imperialist countries are becoming increasingly aware of such maneuvers of global managers. The people of the South in general and the working class in particular are becoming increasingly conscious about the designs of the imperialists and the monopolists.

It is true, reaction has struck the Socialist Europe and the ruling elites there, are conspiring with the global managers of corporate capitalism to hijack their countries to the imperialist camp. But the working classes of these socialist countries will ultimately assert itself, throw out the reactionary elite classes from power and show them their place in history. How quickly and how thoroughly they will do this job entirely depend on the level of understanding and consciousness of the international movement of the working class.

"Working men of all countries unite!" The call of the communist manifesto is even more relevant today than it was some one and a half century ago.

References and Notes

1. This article of "Peter Druckers' 1990s", original published in the Economist appeared in the Economic Times of 27 and 28th October 1989.

2. This item "East—West to North—South" by Edward Mortimer of Financial Times, London appeared in Economic Times of Nov.23rd 1989. The writer speculates on the possible confluence of interests of the West and the Socialist countries and they jointly facing the third world problems.

3. This item "USSR closes ranks with EC" by Malcom Subhan appeared in the Economic Times of 21st December 1989.

4. "Alliances, not competition is the strategy"—article by Francis Cherunilam appeared in Economic Times of 21st Dec. 1989. Report by Quentin Peel of Financial Times, " Radical New Plan f or USSR" appeared in Economic Times of 26th Nov. 1989. The Moscow News of 3rd Dec. 1989 gives an even more graphic picture of this conference where Dr. Abalkin in his key note address presented three alternative proposals for the marketisation of Soviet economy, conservative, radical and moderately radical'. MN reported with regret that none of the three alternatives found acceptance by the delegates who cheered and applauded a fourth alternative which was presented by Alexei Sergeyev, head of a chair at the ALJCTU Higher School of the Trade Union Movement. This fourth alternative was basically for strengthening of the planning mechanism, for confiscation of black money and other related measures which basically rejected the marketisation approach. The conference venue also witnessed demonstrations against " Abalkanisation of the country".

6. The Soviet Monthly "Socialism Principles, Practice and Prospects"—November 1989, where Onikov reviews the progress of Perestroika in an interview to the journal. His comparison of democracy under Brezhnev and Stalin, obviously not meant for justifying Stalin, is neverthess an indicator. It appears that the recent attacks on Stalin are more intended as fight against the economic policies and working class democracy under Stalin rather than for genuine democracy and openness as is generally believed.

RE-ENVISIONING OF SOCIALISM*

Prabhat Patnaik, in his essay on "Re-Envisioning Socialism", endorses the overall vision on socialism that would emerge: However, he insists that the debates on precise modes and problems of transition must wait another occasion. He is inclined to endorse George Lukac's view that, transition to socialism is likely to be long drawn-out, because transition from feudalism to capitalism had taken nearly three centuries. A friend of mine, an IT expert and an enthusiast in the application of Marxism, questions this hypothesis: It ignores the possible impact of the rapidly increasing speed of technological changes.

Facts around the rapidly increasing speed or acceleration of technology were dealt with extensively by several non-Marxian sociologists like the author of Future Shock. And, IT experts have come to believe in the so called Moore's Law, which had predicted doubling of the performance efficiency of electronic chips every two years. Questioning of Patnaik's hypothesis has, therefore, its inherent logic: After all, socialization of material production on a large scale with the help of machines or modern technology, and the impact of technological changes on the society, were at the core of Marx's critique of Capital: Modes and problems of transition, therefore, need to be discussed not in the abstract, but in their specific technological context. The brief commentary, here, is based on such a belief, and a few other points of disagreements with Patanaik, regarding the facts on socialist experience as presented and theorized by him.

Use of machines for material processing and transportation of men and materials across the continents using steam engine and other energy conversion machines, had socialized the process of physical production to unprecedented levels, and at the same time enhanced by several fold, the physical productivity of mankind. Riding on what may be called the *first* industrial revolution, the bourgeoisie classes, all over the world, had created new nation states under their hegemony: However, they were incapable of developing a global political economy or an *integrated and inter-dependant world* thanks to the imperialist interregnum, as rightly theorized by Lenin. Even today, the first industrial revolution has not run its full course, but mankind is already experiencing the impact of a second *industrial revolution,* better known as Information Technology and Communication (IT&C) Revolution, which is socializing and globalizing intellectual production to hitherto unprecedented scale, and enhancing by several fold the intellectual productivity of mankind.

As early as in late fifties, even before the dawn of this second industrial revolution, Professor Galbraith had theorized that, mankind had developed enough of technologies, that could feed and sustain several times the then estimated world population of four billion (Affluent Society, 1958). One may take a view that, those were good enough technological conditions for the practice of socialism, and now the first and second industrial revolutions together have created a technological environment needed for the flowering of communism. Based on the experience of past couple of centuries, one may even theorize that, subjective or ideological factors continue to hold back humanity from taking the plunge in pursuit of socialism and communism.

Visions of an integrated and interdependent world of Perestroika days had an objective technological basis, but they failed to recognize the harsh reality of imperialism, working overtime to subvert socialism. With the down fall of socialist camp, capital which owns and control the means of production, material as well as intellectual, has come to occupy the central stage of global politics once again, taking imperialism to new heights of hegemony, exploitation and oppression. Re-envisioning of socialism need to be thought of, not in the abstract, but in this given historical context, when social and political contradictions are sharpening by the day with increasing momentum, and global capital and bourgeoisie classes or the imperialists are inventing newer and newer methods of bypassing and destroying democracy and democratic values. Their attempts to subvert the UN System and the insistence on substituting it with the IBRD-IMF-WTO trio, are proof enough for their lack of faith in democracy and equality of nationalities, an essential prerequisite for the orderly development of mankind.

The UN system, with its numerous international organizations (including the trio, IBRD-WTO-IMF) spanning nearly the entire spectrum of human endeavor, is a post-Marxian development of great historic significance, which could hardly be ignored by Marxists. The two global wars, in quick succession, had stressed the need for a World Government, if humanity was to survive and benefit from the steadily accelerating technological developments. Bolshevik revolution had recognized the value of League of Nations as a new historical experience, despite its polemics with Trotsky: Soviet Union itself was seen a a mini league of nations, that had liberated the numerous nationalities from centuries old Tsarist oppression, and creating a multinational state that was distinctly different from the old colonial type. Soviet Union could play a leading role in the constitution of UNO, not only as a winner in the second world war, but also as a multinational state with vast experience in managing cultural diversities of continental proportions and the inevitable emotional conflicts, triggered by that devastating war.

Formation of USSR, its heroic survival of the second global war under the proletarian leadership, and its peaceful dissolution, later, into the CIS, as well as the growth and development of UNO and the numerous international institutions created by it, including IBRD, IMF, WTO etc which are now under separate charters, are all important developments that are extremely relevant, while speculating on transition to socialism and global governance. Patnaik has missed this broad canvas while concluding: *"The choice before us today, as it was at the time of Lenin and Luxnburg, is between socialism and barbarism, between a situation where a predatory imperialism remains locked in perennial combat with equally ruthless groups of terrorists, thus threatening the very survival of our civilization, and one that produces both imperialism and its terrorist "other" is overthrown."* This above formulation, along with his doubts expressed on the existence of a general crisis in capitalism, takes away the incentives for any meaningful discussion on 'the precise problems that would arise in the course of transition to socialism'.

'Imperialism which is in perennial combat with terrorism', according to Patnaik, 'is threatening our civilization';

but he has refrained from defining the contours of this contemporary civilization. He does not recognize the intensification of capitalist crisis due to imperialism trying to deepen its stranglehold over the peoples of the developing world, by making use of the rapid technological changes. Neither does he see the resistance against imperialist oppression and exploitation, put in by the two hundred or so nation states of the developing world. He makes no mention about the struggle by the peoples of developing countries against imperialism and their collaborators. Patnaik has not cared to look at the possibilities for joint initiatives of developing countries, regional as well as global, as in the very recent past, against imperialist exploitation and oppression. He rules out the possibility of intra-imperialist rivalry breaking out in any serious manner, based on an extremely unrealistic perception of global politics. Patnaik has constructed a world with imperialists and terrorists as the sole active players; that have nothing to do with the real world of ours. Such a perception has nothing to do with the basic formulations on the four principal contradictions of our epoch, as spelt out in the 1960 Moscow declaration by 61 communist parties: Most working class parties of the World, including the CPI(M), of which Patnaik is a member, hold them to be relevant even today, despite the disintegration of the USSR and the collapse of socialist camp. And, as Lenin had prophesied: . . . . *this one country, thanks to the Soviet power, has done so much that even if the Soviet power in Russia were to be crushed by world imperialism tomorrow, . . . it would still be found that Bolshevik tactics have brought enormous benefit to socialism and have assisted the growth of the invincible world revolution. (Lenin-Proletarian Revolution and Renegade Kautsky)*

Patnaik has discussed, at length, issues related to democracy, organizational principles and democratic centralism, as practiced under 'old socialism'. Intention here is not challenging the numerous facts he had presented but to supplement them, which incidentally could lead to altogether different perceptions about 'old socialism'. He is right in complementing Lenin for suffering open dissent by Bucharin and others *even during the most difficult post-revolutionary times . . . . The question of silencing them through disciplinary action never arose. Such silencing of dissent was a later and altogether unwholesome development.* This fact is of great relevance to the conduct of ideological polemics, within the Indian revolutionary movement, which on occasions degenerate into Pol Potism of the worst kind. However, it need to be noted that, the so called silencing of dissent had only started, several years after Lenin's death. There was a prolonged ideological and political struggle led by Stalin against the so called opposition within and outside the Bolshevik party, under much more difficult internal situation. It is only fair to concede that Stalin had continued with the democratic traditions of Lenin, under even more hostile environment. True, there were trials and executions: They were part of the then existing global culture which was tolerant even towards war and mass killings, universally abhorred today on simple moral grounds. However, inner party democracy and democratic centralism within the Bolshevik movement did not come to a dead-end, with the demise of Lenin: It has survived not only Stalin, but also several other General Secretaries of CPSU. Without that type of inner-party democracy, it would have been simply impossible for the Soviet Society to survive the hostile encirclement of imperialism and to register the great achievements of the Soviet Union in war and in peace.

In support of the hypothesis that, inner party democracy was alive and kicking within the CPSU even after Lenin, one may quote from Onikov (a CC Member of CPSU and staunch supporter of Perestroika), regarding inner party democracy in the party organisation of Moscow region: *Up to 1940 there was not a single case at dozens of its [party of Moscow region] of a nominee for full or candidate membership of the regional or city party committee or the auditing commission being elected unanimously. It was a common practice then, especially in the 1920's, that some of the candidates were not elected. The first case when all nominees for full or candidate membership of the regional committee and the auditing committee were elected unanimously was reported in 1974; not a single nominee in the voting list was voted down. In 1976, the same happened at the city conference (Onikov-Soviet Monthly, Socialism Principles Practice and Prospects-November 1989).* It may be noted that, Onikov had assembled this data in order to discredit Brezhnev & Co and not for supporting Stalin.

Rise and fall of Khrushchev are themselves sufficient proof for the healthy practice of democratic centralism within CPSU: Future historians are sure to make a more balanced view on the degeneration of democracy and democratic centralism within the CPSU, and may trace its beginnings to Khrushchev's revisionist reforms of 1961, implemented slowly but steadily by the intellectual classes of the Soviet Union, despite resistance put up by the working people. These reforms were intentioned to take away the political supervision of economic enterprises and to bring them under the bureaucratic care and control of the intelligentsia. This writer had experienced, in person, the debates on Ota Sik reforms in socialist Czechoslovakia during 1964-65; with engineers and other sections of intelligentsia on one side, supporting the reform and the workers and TU leaders opposing it at the grass root level. Heat of this debate was felt even at far off Tiruchirappalli, within the tiny Czechoslovak community that had come over to India, for setting up the boiler factory of BHEL. This conflict within Czechoslovak society was real and part of a democratic process within, and not a creation of 'Soviet Imperialism', as alleged at that time by the bourgeoisie media. Ota Sik reforms were later temporarily withdrawn and Dubcek, like Khrushchev, was forced to bow out under pressure from the working class.

It is natural that, class contradictions and class perceptions do not disappear even after long years of building socialism. Overlooking these social realities, while reforming or re-designing of systems of governance or management of economic enterprises, are sure to end up as fatal mistakes. Bolshevik revolution had established a system of governance and management of public institutions based on grass root level democracy, where the working people, their collectives and trade unions had played the key role, and not necessarily the intellectual classes and traditional bureaucracy. Even special schools and evening classes were opened, during Stalin's time, for training up ordinary workers and their children to take up key occupations within a short time. Special Universities were opened for ending, within a short time, the monopoly hold of aristocracy over intellectual occupations. This sort of built-in class bias in the management of street-level public institutions and human resources development had naturally attracted criticism and opposition from intellectual classes, reflections of which could be seen in the literary works of Pasternak, Solzhenitsyn and several others. Reforms by Ota Sik, Khrushchev and Gorbachev had a common objective: end of grass root level democracy and politics. Gorbachev had finally succeeded in banning politics from work places: By that time even party organizations at the higher levels were brought under the control of intellectual classes, as indirectly conceded by Patnaik: *a person could become the general secretary of the CPSU without believing in socialism!*

Legally enforceable guarantees on right to work and related fundamental rights had naturally reinforced the practice of grass-root level democracy in socialist countries,. Workers exercised their right to criticize not only their immediate supervisors, but even the managers of economic enterprises, who were legally bound to discuss all aspects of production planning, including questions of quality, productivity improvements and compensation packages, with the trade unions and in the shop floor level joint management committees. Industrial democracy, as practiced today in Western Europe, came into existence as an inevitable response to the shop-floor democracy practiced, extensively in East European countries, next door. For example, joint stock companies of West Germany were brought under legal compulsion to constitute joint management boards with equal representation for the workers and the Board of Directors elected by the shareholders and these laws continue to be valid even today. Enterprises managers in West Europe are legally obliged to consult trade unions not only on policy issues but also to share with them complete information on business performance. As West Europe tried to copy the principles of participative management and industrial democracy that were widely practised in the socialist block Japan was inspired by the massive voluntary movement of innovators and inventors, jointly organized by workers and technologists on the shop floor and then coordinated as part of the socialist initiative at the national level. During the post-war years, these voluntary movements originating from the shop floors of Soviet Union were widely adopted by East European countries: They were then re-christened as Quality Circles (QC) in Japan, under the guidance of Professor Deming of the Harvard University.

Management theorists and market economists in the payrolls of the bourgeoisie could be hardly expected to confess on the lessons they had learnt from the great socialist experiments in governance and enterprises management. Nevertheless, it is quite legitimate to conclude that, unlike in USA, monopoly capitalism in Western Europe and Japan had adopted, in large measure, the enterprises management methods developed by Soviet Union and other socialist countries that were based on grass root level democracy. And, contrary to the false propaganda by imperialists and bourgeoisie intellectuals, Science and Technology in Soviet Union and the socialist block had experienced quantum jumps, thanks to these democratic methods of management that could draw heavily from the creativity of people, who were liberated from the yoke of capitalist oppression. Debates on the relative roles of democracy and bureaucracy in enterprises management and economic management in socialist countries were grossly one-sided in the past, and continue to be ill-informed: Theories and perceptions on convergence by Galbraith did not find supporters on either side of the ideological divide, thanks to the ideological blinkers and rigidities of the cold war environment. The essay on Re-envisioning of Socialism cannot claim to be an exemption from this general trend.

Patnaik had commented that, old socialism, especially in its later years, had appealed to the self interests of the workers and not to their social commitments: *Old socialism depoliticized the workers. Our vision of the socialism of the future must entail a resurrection of politics, a perennial engagement with the politics on the part of the working class, which will also provide the answer to the problem of work motivation in socialist societies.* He is right when he insists that, this cannot be ensured by adopting a religious approach to Marxism. Nevertheless, the question need to be asked and honestly answered: Who, at what point of time, and which forces within or outside the socialist societies, had depoliticized the workers and how?

Re-envisioning of socialism demands not only the right answers to these vital questions, but also a comprehensive understanding of the ongoing globalization under the impact of the second industrial revolution, and of the international organizations that have already come into existence within and outside of the UNO, as well as their potential role in a future system of global governance. Discourses, that neglect these objective realities, are not only un-Marxian but also counterproductive.

* Published in the Economics and Political Weekly of August 16, 2008 as a response to "Re-Envisioning Socialism" by Prabhat Patnaik, published in the same journal on November 3, 2007.

STATE AND THE KNOWLEDGE WORKER

Peter Drucker, considered the guru of corporate capitalism, was the first to use terminologies like, knowledge worker, knowledge society, knowledge economy etc. He had even theorized that Knowledge Workers have created a post-capitalist society, driven by Knowledge rather than Capital.

This paper examines such hypothesizes in the context of contemporary realities and argues that, state power guided and tempered by politics is the deciding factor in business or economic development, over which Knowledge Workers have little or no influence.

Evolution of Indian State as well as its strengths and weaknesses are then examined in this global backdrop. Considerable institutional capacities, technological and managerial, were created after national independence, at the federal or central level.

However, Indian State continues to be weak and poorly organized, compared to its counterparts in developed countries. State Governments are grossly underdeveloped, and local self governments with two employees per thousand population on the average, compared to fifty seven in the USA, hardly exist.

Strengthening the federal foundations of the Centre, and inducting more knowledge workers into local self government institutions are suggested as urgent remedies, if Indian society is to benefit from knowledge workers and the so called paradigm shift to Public Private Participation.

Consultancy is a highly creative profession. Unlike writers, consultants deal with living characters, both men and organizations, rather than their abstractions from past or for future: product is a symphony produced and delivered for once, and hardly amenable for replays. Consultancy today, is a flourishing trade, globally. Even a new tribe of political consultants, reminiscent of the era of Rajagurus and Kautilya, have appeared on the horizon. They played a key role in the downfall of Soviet Union and the disintegration of what was once known as the Socialist Block. Even religion is transforming itself into spiritual consultancy, transcending even national boundaries and substantially contributing to the invisibles in national income statements. Consultants help the client to develop a vision and to realize the dreams associated with it: The client could be an individual, an organization, or even a local or national government.

Consultancy Business is mostly owned by the top layers of Knowledge Workers. Peter Drucker, the Guru of twentieth century corporate management, had coined the phrase of Knowledge Workers (KW) in 1959, in order to describe the managerial classes in the pay rolls of corporations, owned by entrepreneurs and finance institutions. He differentiated this class of wage earners from their fellow proletarians in a much later 1988 essay, Management and the World's Work: *'When Marx was beginning work on Das Kapital in the early 1850s, the phenomenon of management was unknown. So were the enterprises that managers run. The largest manufacturing company around was a Manchester, England cotton mill employing fewer than 300 people, owned by Marx's friend and collaborator Frederick Engels. And in Engel's mill-one of the most profitable businesses of its day-there were no "managers," only first-line supervisors , or charge hands, who were workers themselves, each enforcing discipline over a handful of fellow 'proletarians'* [1]. According to him, *'in less than 150 years management had transformed the social and economic fabric of developed countries and has created a global economy and set new rules for countries that would participate in that economy as equals'.* The new class of KW, according to his perceptions, has liberated itself from finance and investment capital and developed an existence even outside the corporations they managed.

Knowledge economy or post-capitalist economy, driven by an autonomous class of KW, was a favourite theme of many management experts of late eighties and early nineties; a trend vastly encouraged by the rapid strides in information and communication technologies (ICT). In 1989, Drucker himself had predicted in another famous article, Peter Drucker's 1990s: *'Business tomorrow will follow two new rules: One: to move work to where the people are, rather than people to where the work is. Two: to farm out activities that do not offer opportunities for advancements into fairly senior management and professional positions (e.g. clerical work, maintenance, the "Back office" in the brokerage house, the drafting room in the large architectural firm, the medical lab in the hospital) to an outside contractor. The corporation, in stock market jargon, will be unbundled'.* True, Businesses Process Outsourcing (BPO) has taken place in a big way and it has not yet lost its momentum: Even a sort of Knowledge Process Outsourcing (KPO) has emerged which is closer to external consulting by business organizations. With the rapid developments of ICT in recent years, it was fashionable with most futurologists, to speculate on an emerging virtual economy or e-economy on a global scale, based on concepts like e-business, e-banking, e-money and the like, transcending the boundaries of even national economies.

However, the theories of knowledge economy, centred around the new class of KW, found little acceptance in developed market economies which continued to be navigated by the profit motive of capital, which was turning more and more speculative: global corporations continue to expand across the seven continents along the traditional trajectories set by political and market-economists. True, their ownership and management are distinctly different from the days of East India Companies and their successors like Rockefeller, Morgan, Carnegie, Krupp and other typical capitalists who could finance their industries, apparently out of their own pockets and they as individuals had owned and controlled what Marx had qualified as **the means of production.** Today, modern corporations in OECD countries are mostly owned by pension and insurance funds of working people and other financial institutions, which are closely regulated by Governments. They are managed by professionals or knowledge workers and specialists. Individual capitalists, like prehistoric dinosaurs, are extinct today in developed economies: However, they have staged a comeback in former socialist countries and less developed market economies like India [2.]

True, the KW of Drucker play a key role in managing modern corporations as well as the management of financial institutions that own them, either as employees of these organizations or as professional consultants and civil servants. Transformation of capitalist enterprises into knowledge based enterprises and that of market economy into welfare economy etc, as theorized by management consultants, were truly a post-war phenomenon. However, these transformations were the product of policy initiatives at the political plane, initially in USA by President Franklin Roosevelt and then in other OECD countries, based on the Keynesian theories of welfare economics. In fact, even before the Second World War, Soviet Union had started experimenting with its own model of welfare economics, under the system of socialist planning, which essentially was a knowledge-based system for managing a welfare economy based on universal and compulsory social security, pension and insurance schemes for the entire people. These initiatives by the Soviet State had transformed Tsarist Russia and its colonial dependencies into a modern industrial country that could challenge even the war machine of Nazi Germany, the then industrial superpower of Europe. This transformation was the handiwork of Soviet Revolution, which had developed a vision of its own with the help of knowledge workers groomed by it. According to Prof Galbraith and other liberal economists the two models of the so-called post-capitalist society, though apparently confronting each other in cold-war, were in fact converging and even learning from each other, with regard to the role of knowledge workers in managing business and government [3].

World Development Report 1997 with its focus on *'The State in Changing World'* had noted: *'Over the last century the size and scope of government have expanded enormously, particularly in the industrial countries'* [4.] According to WDR estimates, total government expenditure in OECD countries was less than ten percent of their GDP in 1870. This had steadily grown five fold, to nearly fifty percent by 1995. Critics of market economics had pointed out even earlier that, State had continued to grow in these countries even during eighties and nineties, despite the tall talks of Thatcherism and Reagnomics, and had held this in support of their theories on State Monopoly Capitalism and Industrial-Military complexes. Expansion and enrichment of the role of State, on either side of the cold war, was characterized as proof of convergence of socio-political systems, by Professor Galbraith and other liberal economists. State played a key role in the development of national economies of OECD countries, not only in social welfare and national defence but also in the development of hard core technologies related to electric power and energy, nuclear and fossil fuels, rail and road transport, ship building, space, communications and numerous other sectors of economic activity. State in the developed countries has in its roll the best among Knowledge Workers for playing this key role and also uses the services of private consultants and consultancy organizations to work for them. It is to be noted that the State was engaging consultants or knowledge workers even outside the public domain, for performing certain well defined duties and functions decided as part of a political process or consensus. It was the Government or the State that was calling the shots, based on a democratic consensus in these countries, and not the Knowledge Workers.

Marx had looked at the State mostly as an instrument of oppression by ruling classes. However, newly liberated countries like India, inspired by the success of the Soviet model as well as the prevalent practices in Western democracies, had looked at the institution of State as a critical resource for social progress and economic development. According to the WDR-1997 quoted earlier, central government expenditure in developing countries was just fifteen percent of their GDP in 1960 which had nearly doubled up by 1990. In the Indian economy, total government expenditure had peaked to 26 percent of GDP by 1991 and then started declining, thanks to the economic reforms. It was argued that, due to economic planning and growth of public sector organizations, India was over-administered, and down-sizing of Government at every level was recommended as the first necessary step toward faster growth of the national economy. Fallacy of this argument will be clear, when we consider the numerical size of Governments in industrial countries: USA with a population base of 265 million had 24 million Government employees in 2002, including its armed forces, or some 91 employees per 1000 population. India with 1100 Million people had only 13 million Government employees or about twelve per thousand populations [5]. India is a thinly administered country by any standard, combined with lower efficiencies at every level Indian State is no match to that of the USA. Even a casual look at the two societies will reinforce this statistical evidence. Table-1 compares the relative strength and distribution of public employees in India and USA at the three levels of Government: Federal or Centre, State and Local.

TABLE-1
EMPLOYEES PER 1000 POPULATION: YEAR 2002
Excluding autonomous institutions and public enterprises

	USA	INDIA
Federal/Central Govt.	20	3
State Governments	19	7
Local Governments	52	2
Total	91	12

A recent report from South Africa, which had a fairly extensive state apparatus, developed during the Apartheid regime, illustrates the impact of downsizing of government on the efficacy of governance: *'A consultant fretting about constant consultancy across government agencies is like South African Breweries calling for abstinence, but we seem to be reaching a stage where we can only master the public sector's nagging capacity challenge by thinking the previously unthinkable. In some parts of the government the call on outside advisers is perennial and dependency is setting in. Yet consultancy should be a support function, not the core driver of departmental outputs. Consultancy firms enjoy the fee income, but some privately acknowledge that a credibility crisis is looming for departments that seem unable to stand on their own feet and consultants who seem unable to make a difference . . . . Annual staff turnover in critical skills and management categories runs at an estimated 20% to 30%. A consultant may work intensely with a team, build competence and get good results from high performers. By year-end, staff turnover may have removed the entire managerial layer. The consultant starts again and is sometimes the only provider of continuity.'* (Business Day of Johannesburg 22nd Oct 2007. S Asbury, CEO of Gemini Consulting). Dwindling capacity of government departments to absorb even the marginal outputs from external consultants because of staff attrition, is a common experience with most African countries that have taken to the reform path. Marginalization of the State has been reported from other African countries as well, resulting in lawlessness and misery on a large scale. And, Latin American countries are experiencing, today, a massive swing away from the regime of global consultants and they are resorting to more extensive state intervention and regulation.

Experience of the erstwhile socialist block tells us a different story. KW had occupied a pre-eminent position in the political economy of erstwhile socialist countries. By the early nineties they, as a class, had virtually taken over the control of state apparatus, in Soviet Union and other East European countries, thanks to the reforms initiated by Khrushchev in the early sixties. KW were already occupying key positions in the Government, the national economy and also in the Communist Party of Soviet Union, when Gorbachev initiated his perestroika and glasnost movement in 1987, with the noble objective of enriching the democratic content of its socialist regime. Within three or four years, KW or the so called intelligentsia could hijack the reform movement, remove Gorbachev from power, dismantle Soviet Union, and bring Russia under the dictatorship of Yeltsin who is now hated by the entire people of Russia and most CIS countries. The so called Western Aid for introducing market reforms in Soviet Union was mostly subsumed by the cleverer among the Russian KW as consultancy fees: They used these fraudulent incomes for acquiring the controlling shares of the massive Soviet enterprises for a song, and President Putin is now trying to salvage an embezzled economy. Situation is not different in other CIS and East European countries. However, despite its massive reform programs, China has so far refused to weaken the role of the State or to demobilize its massive public enterprises and initiatives. And, using these public sector resources, it continues to make best use of the services of even global consultants.

Import of consultancy was virtually restricted to technology transfer in the regulatory regime that came into existence in our country, as part of the Industrial Development Act of 1951. These restrictions were in place until 1991, when liberalization of the Indian economy was initiated on a large scale. Departments of the Central Government, Indian Railways, institutions like Planning Commission along with its numerous working groups, Central Water & Power Commission, Central Electricity Authority, Atomic Energy Commission, ISRO and the numerous other public sector enterprises specializing in various sectors like SAIL, CIL, ONGC, GAIL, EIL, IOC, BHEL, NTPC and several other specialist organizations had doubled up as consultants to the nation on various sectors of the national economy. Most of these capabilities were built on the strength of international cooperation, supplemented and strengthened by bilateral trade agreements with OECD countries as well as the socialist block. The large public enterprises of the Central Government had served as technology generators of the nation for more than four decades and several of them were declared as autonomous Navaratna companies, considering their strategic importance. These organizations and enterprises along with the S&T Institutions under CSIR, ICMR, ICAR, DSIR and other Central Government departments had developed the core consultancy capabilities needed for a developing economy.

Mixed economy of our Union Republic was a bold and innovative experiment in a country of continental proportions with unity and in diversity written large on its cultural signpost: Nehru had called it the tryst with destiny of the Indian people. Institutional capabilities built up by the Central Government, within a couple of decades of national independence, were indeed formidable with their large contingents of scientists, engineers, technologists, planners, economists, social scientists and numerous other categories of knowledge workers. National economy had experienced rapid growths in several sectors, like grid power development, fuel production and prospecting, steel, aluminium, nuclear energy, power equipment, machine building, communication, space, transportation, heavy machine building etc. Despite the lingering problems of poverty, the country could achieve food-security, improve the quality of life in general and sustain a parliamentary democracy considered to be the largest in the world. True, national economy as a whole could hardly cross the traditional Hindu rate of growth and our massive capacity building program in government, embarked after national independence, had its blind spots.

Basic weakness in our capacity building strategy was possibly its over-centralization: Everything was built around Delhi and in conformity with its imperial tradition. CSIR, ICAR, ICMR, CWC and most other national institutions did not have their state level counterparts that could impart these national institutions a genuinely federal character. Problems of industrial development, health, food and agriculture or water resources development have their sub-national dimensions which were very well recognized in our constitution that had divided governmental powers into water-tight compartments, violating the traditionally federal character of Indian polity. For example, when in 1989, the Inland Waterways Authority of India (IWAI) was formed; there was a proposal to set up a Kerala Inland Waterway Authority (KIWA) to work as its subsidiary or joint venture, to take on the responsibility of developing the 1700 Km of inland waterway potential of Kerala, which is noted for its unique hydrological features [6.]

The 160 Km long Kollam-Kottapuram National Waterway-III was seen as a political gift from Delhi and IWAI has been spending millions of Rupees every year on this project for the past two decades: However, the structures created by them remain grossly underutilized, because of defective conceptualization and lack of involvement and participation by local communities. In sharp contrast, the Cochin International Airport Ltd (CIAL), a company closely held by Kerala Government, has recently built a highly cost effective international airport, which is the envy of most non-metro airports in the country. CIAL was immensely benefited by the professional expertise of Airport Authority of India (AAI) with its vast experience in building airports in India and abroad for nearly half a century. Cochin airport is often wrongly projected as a successful example of Public Private Participation: But, it was virtually a joint venture of AAI and CIAL, two public sector organizations [7.]

In the good old days, Planning Commission, and its numerous working groups had served as the forum for policy making and producing consensus, at the national or federal level. ONGC and GAIL along with other public sector oil companies could help the central government to decide on a federal petroleum policy in the best interests of the country as whole. The Central Electricity Authority along with the State Electricity Boards served as a federal planning and policy making platform, which had helped in increasing the per capita generation and consumption of electricity several fold, a growth rate that could not be sustained by the slow moving national economy. All these are now changed, or are rapidly changing under the impact of reforms. The planning process has been diluted and the central government has mostly withdrawn from its policy making and program formulation responsibilities.

State governments are ill-equipped to fill in the vacuum created by the withdrawal of centre and are at the mercy of external consultants who has no feel about the ground realities at the grass root level. Several mega project concepts were developed during the last decade with the help of foreign consultants: Most of them are stuck up for lack of objectivity and vision while formulating them. Even the much talked about Special Economics Zones, supposedly under the control of Central Government on territories liberated from state governments, are failing to take off. Individual state governments and local bodies are being advised to directly negotiate loans from multilateral agencies for infrastructure development and they simply do not have the expertise or capability to take on such responsibilities. Capacity building exercises, modernization in government programs and e-governance programs taken up by Kerala government and funded by multilateral agencies had met with little success: Experience in this regard is close to that of South Africa, already referred to in an early paragraph.

This, possibly, is the experience with most state governments and the Central Government is aware of their disabilities and utter lack of professionalism in their dealings. It appears that the government departments at the centre have little faith in the professional capabilities of their counterparts at the state level. The draft eleventh plan has proposed allotment of plan funds directly to the districts and local bodies, bypassing the state governments. However, it is common knowledge that, most centrally sponsored program had failed in the past because of bureaucratic approaches and faulty delivery systems at the grass root level and because of weak or non-existent local governments. Peoples Planning Program of Kerala Government during the 1996-2001 period had sought to overcome this difficulty by deploying a large number of volunteers trained up by the State Planning Board. Dozens of handbooks and manuals were produced and crash programs organized for developing thousands of barefoot consultants, who were looked down and instantly rejected as political commissars by the working people. And within a year of their deployment they produced an inventory of about 100,000 project reports: bulk of them is dead and declared useless. The program has taught us a valuable lesson that the problems of inadequate governance cannot be overcome, simply by deputing low cost barefoot consultants.

We had seen from Table-1 that governance at all levels is extremely weak in India, compared to that in USA, a typical modern state, we all try to emulate. In terms employees per 1000 population, US Federal Government was nearly seven times stronger. State Governments in USA had nearly three times more employees compared to Indian States on a population basis. Local Self Governments, with less than two employees per thousand people, are the weakest links of State power in India. They are mere pygmies compared to their US compartments, which constitute a formidable part of US State power. With 52 employees per 1000 population, local governments in USA are the providers of a variety of community services at the street level: education, health, social security, human resources development, local transport, trade, tourism etc. Despite the Gandhian dreams of Gram-Swaraj, the JP movement of seventies, constitutional amendments of 1991 and repeated demands and promises by the Left and the Right, Local Governments are a virtual non-starter in our Union Republic.

Governments, at the state as well as local level, need the support of external consultants in a big way. Even the barefoot consultants engaged by them could do a lot and take the multitudes of our people to modernity and progress, faster and in a much more wholesome manner than the voluntary and non-governmental organizations. However, the more fundamental question is how they could build up the minimum of governing capabilities? It is a political question to be dealt by Indian democracy.

---

*   This was written in 2009 for "Consulting Ahead", the mouth piece of Consultancy Development Centre of Government of India

NOTES:

1.   Managers and Marx: Drucker and other management theorists often argue that industrial management, technology etc are purely post-Marxian developments. They conveniently forget that impact of technology on the relations of production was the subject of inquiry of Das Kapital: Sufficient to mention here, the titles of two chapters of Volume I of Capital: Chapter XIV Division of labour and manufacture, and Chapter XV-Machinery and modern

industry. Size of Engel's' factory is irrelevant here, because that was not the sole source of wisdom for Marx and his followers.

2. ndividual capitalists: Individual capitalists are extinct in almost all developed countries; they sound like prehistoric animals even in the Indian context. Capitalist economy is driven by capital in the abstract or the capitalist class, and not by individual capitalists. This basic issue is often overlooked by management experts while evaluating the efficacy of market economies.

3. John Kenneth Galbraith of Harvard University was a pioneer in liberal economics and had assembled his non-conventional economic thoughts in his famous book Affluent Society (1958) in which he had attacked what he called conventional wisdom of economists, in pursuit of blind growth and consumerism. He had sought values beyond GDP estimates and had disagreed with the consumerist tendencies in socialist economies. He had noted the parallel movements in the economies of divergent ideologies, in support of his theory of convergence. Galbraith and his followers were initially enthusiastic about the reforms of Gorbachev, but had always doubted the efficacy of his plans to build a market economy from the scratch.

4. World Development Report-1997: Theme of this report was The State in a Changing World. It looked at the evolution of State and its institutions over the past century and its role in social and economic development. Experience of different systems including that of Soviet Union and other socialist countries are the subject of discussion and analysis.

5. Size of Governments: The data presented here was compiled by the author from various sources and an analysis based on this study was published in the Passline of 15th September 2005 under the title: Globalization and downsizing of governments.

6. Kerala Inland Water Authority: Kerala is a narrow strip of land with a 560 Kilometre coastline on the West, and mountain relief on the East. Every 14 kilometre on the average, there is a river system flowing westward, and forty-one drainage basins rush their heavy monsoon run-off, into a huge inland water body, stretching along the coastline and shaking hands with the Arabian Sea, at half a dozen locations called pozhi. Administration of this water body is in poor shape. The KIWA suggestion was made by this author, in his capacity as Government Secretary for Public Enterprises in 1988, when IWAI was formed with the late Xavier Arrakkal Ex-MP as Chairman. The unique hydrology of Kerala had provoked our former President to suggest the development of a comprehensive smart waterway for the Kerala coast.

7. CIAL: Possibly the first airport company in the world. It is often projected as an example for PPP. However, private equity participation is nominal. CIAL has a BoD with Kerala Chief Minister as Chairman and dominated by ministers and bureaucrats. Success of this venture was the cooperation and collaboration with the Airport Authority of India. This sort of Centre-State joint initiative has proved to be a far better route, compared to joint ventures with private investors and this experience has influenced the new policy announcements on airport development.

BANGLADESH AND ITS PRIVATE UNIVERSITIES*

Bangladesh with its 150 million people, and bordered by eight Indian states including West Bengal, is a neighbor of great economic, social and cultural significance for India. It is a densely populated country and as in Kerala, nearly a third of its geographical area is covered by water bodies. Rice and vegetable cultivation, agro-processing industries, inland fisheries, inland water transport, water tourism and higher education are obvious areas for mutual cooperation and trade between Kerala and Bangladesh. The author was in Bangladesh for more than a week visiting the International University for Business, Agriculture and Technology (IUBAT), a pioneering private university in Dhaka.

The two Bengals, East and West together, have a population close to 230 million. Dhaka, the second populous city of the subcontinent and next only to Kolkata, is the capital of the Peoples Republic of Bangladesh, which has nearly three times the population of Kerala. And, Dhaka is just 520 Km away from Kolkata by road, which is getting connected by rail, hopefully by the next Ramzdan season. Most part of my column, this month, was done, sitting in Dhaka: I was invited by the International University for Agriculture, Business and Technology (IUBAT), as a Senior Visiting Fellow. Prof Dr. Alimullah Miyan, the leader of the non-Government university movement in Bangladesh, a friend and associate of mine, had founded this non-government university in 1991, the first of its kind in Bangladesh.

Peoples of the subcontinent have completed this year sixty years of independence, from the more than two centuries of colonial rule. However, there were no signs of grand celebrations in any part of the subcontinent. In India, the ruling United Progressive Alliance, despite the long patriotic traditions of its leading constituent, the Indian National Congress, was on the defensive on the Indo-US nuclear treaty: The treaty has allegedly compromised on national sovereignty. In Pakistan, where independence day is observed on August 14th, US administration was advising President Mushrraf to share political power with his rivals, Benazir Bhuto and Navaz Shariff. Bangladesh celebrates its independence day on 26th March to mark the victory of its liberation army against Pakistani occupation: War of liberation had lasted more than seven months, cleansing not only its cities and towns but also its villages; and Sheik Mujibr Rehman founded the Peoples Republic of Bangladesh on the 26th March of 1971. Founder of the republic was, however, shot dead on the 15th August 1974: Despite the long standing demands from peoples from all walks of like, Bangladesh establishment has not cared to dedicate the day in memory of this great martyr. During the week around August 15th, English newspapers of Dhaka were abundant with articles and reviews on the sixty years of partition and Mujib's martyrdom. Inevitably all of them reflected the yearnings of the peoples of the subcontinent to live in peace and harmony, despite religious and cultural differences.

Islam is the majority religion (88%) of Bangladesh with Hindus in a minority (11%): Like India, it is a secular republic. Buddhism had dominated the region in good old days, and there are several ancient Buddhist enclaves all over the republic. Bangladesh is totally bordered by Indian States, the so-called seven sisters of the North-East and then its own Hindu version on the West: On the South is a short coast line of some 140 Km of the Indian Ocean. Metros of Dhaka and Kolkata share identical cultural traditions and the two regions of Bengal have, by and large, an exemplary past of religious harmony. West Bengal was developing as a member state of Indian Union for the past six decades and Bangladesh as an independent country, after its liberation from Pakistan in 1971. Cultural and linguistic sentiments are far more predominant in Bangladesh: Number plates of motor vehicles are in Bengali like most sign boards on street and boulevards. Tagore's "Amar Sonar Bangla"is its national anthem. Tagore himself, as well as several other Bengali celebrities like JC Bose the famous scientist, Amarthya Sen the world renowned economist, magical wizard Sarcar and several others hail from East Bengal and Bangladesh citizens are proud of this common legacy.

People of Bangladesh are far more passionately fired by patriotism, compared to their Indian neighbors. However, their state policies seem to be hardly supportive of such deep patriotic sentiments. Its bureaucracy, as in India and in several other developing countries, largely leans on the West and multilateral agencies dominated by it. The UNIDO and other UN agencies have a much larger presence in Bangladesh compared to India and the country makes much better use of this international cooperation. A typical sector is flood control and disaster management: Bangladesh has developed an extensive flood monitoring system with elaborate field measurement systems, hooked up to a powerful IT network at the national level. The website maintained under the UNDP project provides online information on water levels in the large network of rivers that criss cross Bangladesh territory. This is a far more productive project, compared to the computer literacy and other populist IT programs, perused by several Indian States, including West Bengal and Kerala. However, with regard to industrial development and technological capabilities, Bangladesh visibly lags far behind India, and its economy is driven virtually by imported energy. In energy exploration, power development, and in several areas of frontier as well as traditional technologies, India and Bangladesh could be working together to great mutual advantage. However, there seems to be bureaucratic impediments on either side of the boarder and these have nothing to do with any kind of religious sensibilities or popular sentiments.

Pattern of development in the education system in the two countries is similar: In both countries, higher education is seen by the people, especially the elite classes, as a passport for a decent permanent jobs in the national economy or for migration to developed countries. Medium of education in Universities is English and those in pursuit of upward social mobility prefer English medium schools, right from the Kindergarten. Science and humanity schemes dominate university education, accounting for about 80 percent of total enrollment in the collages affiliated to the public universities. Universities were under the stranglehold of the colonial bureaucracy and even the creation of a University Grants Commission (UGC), soon after liberation, has hardly helped the higher education system to become responsive to the real needs of Human Resources Development as perceived by the society. As Professor Miyan had noted in a recent review paper published in Bangladesh Studies: *"Universities in the country went through a chaotic situation and there was hardly any professionalism in managing the the educational programs prevailing in the universities. The faculty members, generally, were not attentive to their duties; and, in most cases, classes were not held on schedule due to political unrest and in-fighting among the faculty members, the students and administration that created a condition where the universities could hardly function as academic entities . . . ."*

Such critical comments and situations are reflective of the Indian situation as well, and under these suffocating situation in Bangladesh, several academics like Prof Miyan, who were striving to restructure the public universities in Bangladesh, on more rational lines and in the spirit of the national liberation struggles of seventies, saw the opening up of private universities as the only possible step. According to Prof Miyan and his compatriots, the campaign for private universities was a disparate step, and not one of academic adventure. He is critical and conscious about of the commoditization maneuvers by developed countries to create a free global market for higher education as a commodity, when he says: *The challenge for the developing countries is to resist being flooded by second-rate, substandard courses that do not match their cultural setting or socio-economic needs.* The new act for regulating the the establishment of Non-Government Universities passed by Bangladesh National Assembly in 1992 was in pursuit of this undeclared objective and the act was amended once in 1998 in order to improve its efficacy.

Non-Governmental Universities may be seen as the Bangladesh equivalent of India's deemed university scheme administered by its UGC: Working experience of neither appears to have delivered the desired results, despite the progress claimed by their protagonists. Non-Government Universities in Bangladesh are, generally, far more accountable to the students, in completing the courses and conducting examinations on time. Quality of instruction has reportedly improved and curricula rendered more responsive to the real needs of the job market. However such claims of improvements are not uniform and are not reflective of the general experience. Nevertheless there was a massive expansion of private universities in Bangladesh during the past decade. According to UGC statistics there were 53 private universities in the country in 2004 with about 63,000 students. Among those pursuing higher specialist education, six percent went to private universities, eleven percent was with public universities and the balance sought the routine science and humanities streams. However, overseas employment markets continue to distort the entire education system in Bangladesh as well, like in all developing countries including India.

IUBAT founded by Prof Miyan, no doubt, is one of the few success stories among the private university initiatives in Bangladesh, sponsored and promoted by academics: It has consolidated its position during past one and a half decades. IUBAT has exchange programs with over fifty universities abroad, conducts more than a dozen courses in engineering, agriculture and health services, and enrollment has crossed the one thousand mark. It has moved into its own pukka premises, owns ten acres of prime land within the Dhaka development area for its campus, and possesses another one hundred acres of agricultural land in the rural districts earmarked for farm development and research. Most of the universities sponsored by big business have even better records of performance, but there are several others on the decline and under threat of takeover or closure by the UGC bureaucracy. A minimum of land holding and cash reserves in bank are being insisted upon by the Government, in order to ensure solvency of private universities, a proposition that is being resisted by their association: It seems to hold out the view that, fate of non-government universities should be entirely left to the market forces.

And, that hardly is any solution, while considering the larger interests of students and faculty caught under the nightmare of dying universities. Without the guarantees of appropriate safety-nets for the stakeholders, non-governmental universities and other teaching institutions engaged in long-term HRD are sure to lose the much needed credibility. And, education being an essential part of a long-term social process, chance of success is rather remote for partial and isolated reforms. These, in brief, are the lessons from the university reforms of Bangladesh.

---

* Author is a visiting faculty of IUBAT and this article was published in the Passline of August 2007

POLITICAL ECONOMY OF CORPORATE SOCIAL RESPONSIBILITY*

Trusteeship theory of Gandhi had reflected the essence of Corporate Social Responsibility, long long ago. However, there were divergent views on what CSR should aim at, right from the days, when corporate world started defining it: World Business Council for Sustainable Development had defined CSR as "The continuing commitment by business to behave ethically and contribute to economic development while improving the quality of life of the work force and their families as well as of the local community and society at large." Being socially responsible means not only fulfilling legal expectations, but also going beyond compliance; investing in human capital, the environment and in the relations with stakeholders.

Going beyond basic legal obligations in the social sector, could have a direct impact on the productivity of capital. Some CSR consultants believe that, the concept helps in managing social changes with improved competitiveness: They look at CSR not as a philanthropic activity, in which a company gives without expecting a return or a benefit. And, by now, several UN organizations like UNEP, UNIDO and ILO, global congregations like World Social Forum and World Economic Forum, and the numerous country level business organizations and trade union movements had tried at their own definitions: Nevertheless, CSR continues to evade global consensus.

However, one thing is clear from these global debates: CSR makes absolutely no sense under conditions of *laissez-faire*. Possibly, it could make some sense, under a regime of Welfare Capitalism: And, welfare capitalism, as an ideology, was a natural response to Marxian socialism. But, it took long years and two global wars, for a convincingly feasible economic model of welfare state getting acceptance: John Maynard Keynes published his famous book, *The General Theory of Employment, Interest and Money*, in 1936, and Franklin D Roosevelt, the legendary President of USA, was the first statesman to experiment with the Keynesian model, in war and in peace. However, even before Keynes, the Soviets, starting from Lenin's days, had experimented with this basic economic model: Pension and insurance funds of the working people were used for financing the massive five year plans of USSR with resounding success.

One may take the view that, neither Roosevelt nor Keynes was inspired by the Soviet economic model, for any number of reasons: However, the fact remains that, numerous socialist enterprises were managed by professional managers or technocrats, within a non-capitalist or socialist framework. Any discourse on CSR instantly takes me to my younger days, in Czechoslovakia, during early eighties, as an engineer trainee of BHEL (www.bhel. com): I had the opportunity of closely watching how a large socialist enterprise, like the First Brno Engineering Works, specializing in large power boilers, worked in that country. Five year plans and annual plans approved by the ministry were drafted by a Director Board consisting of Trade Union representatives. Shop level components of the plans, including the physical, financial and worker welfare plans, had to be approved by workers' collectives at the grass root level, along with quality and productivity norms. And as I remember, there was a voluntary movement of innovators and inventors in the company, similar to the Japanese Quality Circles promoted under Deming management culture. Even the Brno Municipality, the Local self Government Institution, came in to hold a stake in this century old enterprise, after its nationalization in 1948. Naturally, First Brno was under peer pressure to keep the local environment clean and healthy. As part of its international responsibility First Brno had trained up some two hundred engineers and technicians from India, like myself, in the various aspects of design and construction of power boilers. That was part of an international contract for setting up the boiler plant of BHEL in the far South of the Indian subcontinent. First Brno of early sixties was, in my view, a splendid example for the CSR concept that we discourse today in this international conference.

The culture of industrial democracy that prevailed in Socialist Europe naturally had its impact on the political regime and corporate managements of Western Europe: Professor Galbraith, the great liberal economist of our times, had debated these facts related to post-war corporate management, in support of his theory of convergence of the two apparently divergent political systems (Affluent Society-1956). For example, the German co-determination Act for ensuring workers' participation in management had rendered a very high level of transparency in corporate management in West German PLCs, unlike in US or UK based MNCs. For example as a German stock corporation, Siemens is subject to German corporate law and has a two-tier management and oversight structure, consisting of an eleven member Managing Board and a 20-member Supervisory Board. Let me quote from the annual report of Siemens for 2007: *"The German Co-determination Act (Mitbestimmungsgesetz) requires that the Company's shareholders and its employees each select one-half of the Supervisory Board's members. The Supervisory Board oversees and advises the Managing Board in its management of Company business. At regular intervals, it discusses business development, planning, strategy and implementation. It also discusses Siemens' quarterly and half-yearly reports and approves the annual, stand-alone financial statements of Siemens AG, as well as the Consolidated Financial Statements of Siemens, taking into account both the audit reports provided by the independent auditors and the results of the review conducted by the Audit Committee. It monitors the Company's adherence to statutory provisions, official regulations and internal Company policies (compliance). In addition, the Supervisory Board appoints the members of the Managing Board and allocates members' individual duties".* Important Managing Board decisions—such as major acquisitions, divestments and financial measures—require Supervisory Board approval. In the By-laws for the Managing Board, the Supervisory Board has established rules that govern the work of the Managing Board, in particular the allocation of duties among individual Managing Board members, matters reserved for the Managing Board as a whole, and the required majority for Managing Board resolutions . . . ."* A detailed account of the various committees under these boards and their functions may be seen from the Siemens website (w1.siemens.com).

Such extensive regulations and statutes for social accountability and a highly developed Green movement were strong inhibitors for the development of a separate CSR movement in Germany, which is often branded as a laggard by CSR consultants. Practice of industrial democracy in Western Europe and laws related to employee welfare and participation in management vary from country to country depending on their geographical location and historical background (Industrial Democracy in Europe-Business International 1974 and its updates). However, the more advanced features of industrial democracy in Europe and related statutes in general had guarded against the aggressive entry of US Corporations for a long time. More recently and as part of the WTO reforms and competition laws, insisted on by the USA, country specific concessions and exemptions are being granted to foreign companies: EU has now developed a common frame work on industrial democracy and related statutes. The other centre of welfare capitalism, Japan, has its own ethnic and cultural traits that have opened up in a big way to Deming management philosophy, much more enthusiastically than its country of origin, the USA.

With the collapse of Soviet Union and the Socialist Camp, there was the short lived euphoria over the *end of history* along with ideological polemics and the cold war. Peter Drucker had announced the arrival of *Knowledge Worker* as a class: World Economic Forum and World Social Forum were mobilised by the intellectual classes of the world in support of a *Fourth World* and the so called *sustainable* ideologies. The renewed stress on a globalisation process, based on market economics, had called for not only globally acceptable quality certifications (ISO 14000 etc), but also to adherence to global environmental standards, climate change obligations, and ethical corporate governance, as essential preconditions for competing in the global market. In countries like India, with only a quarter of the population engaged in economic activity and bulk of the working people belonging to the informal sector and living far outside of social security nets, concepts like CSR sounded rather bizarre. Indian businessmen, who aspire for the lucrative markets of the developed countries, even look at CSR *'as tilted in favour of buyers from North and as non-tariff barriers for suppliers from South.'* Nevertheless, several Voluntary Organisations and Consultancy Enterprises have come up in India in recent years, as in the case of environmental impact evaluation and poverty related studies: These services are presently priced modestly at Rs.20,000 (US$ 500) per man-month or even less. And that is not surprising, considering the large stock of educated un-employed in the country.

Unlike the USA with its substantive internal market for goods and services, European nations and Japan are dead keen on exports: Business in these countries have taken to CSR in a big way, as revealed by their classy claims through websites. USA export mostly armaments, software products and IPR and there is hardly any US company making big claims on the CSR front; and the most successful US business of our times, the Microsoft, appears to be a real laggard in this respect, despite Bill Gates' celebrated philanthropic offerings, as he visits third world countries. It appears US business has mindlessly accepted Peter Drucker as its Corporate Guru, who had defined the *first and foremost responsibility of business as making enough profits to cover the costs for the future* (Frontiers of Management 1986). The elaborate anti trust laws and the legendary Ralph Nadar are entities of a bygone era in USA. To quote from a recent report of National Consumers League, America's pioneer consumer organization (www.nclnet.org-founded 1899): *"Eighty two Percent of Americans Want Congress to Ensure Companies Meet Pressing Social Issues. Americans of all political persuasions—96 percent of Democrats, 80 percent of Independents, and 65 percent of Republicans—say that it is either very or extremely important for Congress to ensure that companies are addressing social issues . . . . These findings paint a far different picture of corporate social responsibility than the model laid out by Milton Friedman nearly 40 years ago. The American public not only expects companies to help solve social issues but also wants government to step in to ensure that they do".*

Supporters of free market economy had always frowned on State intervention as an economic sin and looked at self-regulation by sticking to well defined norms of CSR as the panacea for all economic ills. The State was frowned upon as oppressor by both sides of the ideological divide during the cold war, and the so called civil society dominated by the new elite classes of knowledge workers or the intelligentsia, had virtually taken over the responsibility of defining as well as enforcing of CSR concepts. And, NGOs and VOs led by the intelligentsia were inevitably patronised by the Corporates, as an integral part of their CSR. They, in tandem, had looked down at the initiatives and interventions by the public sector. Even the concepts of Nation-States and United Nations Organisation were looked down by massive global formations like World Social Forum or World Economic Forum that had more or less peacefully coexisted with the Breton Woods Institutions that continue to dominate global finance. It was a virtual takeover of the interdependent integrated global village by a global intelligentsia, and a sort of parody of the nineteenth century Marxian appeal: Workers of the World Unite! And the result as we see today, after a free run of two decades of rule by the global intelligentsia is a global financial melt-down!!

Let me conclude this essay with a quote from the last chapter of the celebrated treatise of Keynes, cited in the beginning of this essay: . . . . *But if nations can learn to provide themselves with full employment by their domestic policy, there need be no important economic forces calculated to set the interest of one country against that of its neighbors. There would still be room for the international division of labor and for international lending in appropriate conditions. But there would no longer be a pressing motive why one country need force its wares on another or repulse the offerings of its neighbor, not because this was necessary to enable it to pay for what it wished to purchase, but with the express object of upsetting the equilibrium of payments so as to develop a balance of trade in its own favor. International trade would cease to be what it is, namely, a desperate expedient to maintain employment at home by forcing sales on foreign markets and restricting purchases, which, if successful, will merely shift the problem of unemployment to the neighbor which is worsted in the struggle, but a willing and unimpeded exchange of goods and services in conditions of mutual advantage.*

Keynes was not laying down the rules of competition among nation-states, but sounding the inevitability of planned development and mutual cooperation among them. CSR will render itself socially meaningless, if we forget these Keynesian fundamentals, which was hardly any different from the socialist practices of yesteryears. And, after Keynes, mankind has accumulated the unique historical experience of a United Nations, built on the grand principle of peaceful co-existence of nations and nation-states, and of the numerous international organizations built under its supervision, covering nearly every sphere of human endeavor. Concepts around CSR have to necessarily undergo basic cultural changes under a newly emerging system of global order or global governance.

* Presented in the seminar on Corporate Social Responsibility in Kochi in November 2008, organized by the Institute of Small Enterprises and Development, Kochi Kerala.

CENTRE-STATE RELATIONS AND THE INDIAN LEFT

Central Government, today, is politically weak and lacks in federal authority. Nevertheless, it has inherited from the patriotic years of Nehru-Indira regime, immense administrative powers, even outside of the written constitution. Unity in diversity is the hallmark of Indian polity: however, following the footsteps of British imperialism, India's ruling elite continues to hold our diverse nationalities as prisoners and block their natural development. Left is running a big political risk in neglecting these ground realities and by legitimizing the present Delhi regime with its parliamentary support.

This article written in 2005 was first published in Red Star the mouth piece of CPI(ML). Later, in the same year, Mathrubhoomi a literary weekly published a Malayalam translation. Later, part of the article relating to S&T administration was reproduced in Malayalam in Marxist Samvaadam.

Nationality question and center-state relations.

Human development as a collective endeavor, from family to territorial communities and then to tribes and nationalities is historically well documented. Marxism-Leninism provides the best of tools for understanding the destiny of Man and the evolution of nations and nationalities. Leading social classes had built up nation states, using their economic and military prowess. Industrial revolution and rapid development of Science and Technology (S&T) had led to massive socialization of material and intellectual production, expansion of commerce, as well as expansion and consolidation of nation states ruled by bourgeoisie classes.

Capital of Marx was the first comprehensive appraisal of the impact of modern technology on social and cultural development of mankind. Communist Manifesto had ventured to speculate on a destiny for mankind that transcended time, space and nationalities, and seeking a sort of immortality on the strength of collective existence and technological capabilities (1). However, Lenin had ruled out the possibility for a global unity of nationalities under bourgeoisie rule, which was based on private ownership of the means of production.

For more than two centuries, imperialist wars had blocked human progress in all seven continents: First World War had convinced humanity on the need for a League of Nations for the peaceful coexistence of nations, and for the orderly development of humanity. Lenin had attached great importance to this particular feature of postwar developments. He had described Czarist Russia as a prison of nationalities. Lenin had looked at the liberation and full development of the numerous nationalities and sub-nationalities oppressed by Czar, as a necessary precondition for the success and sustainability of Bolshevik revolution, under the leadership of Russian proletarians. The USSR itself was a mini League of Nations, and served as a model for the working together of peoples of diverse ethnic origin, culture and nationality and seeking a common destiny. The extensive UN System (2) of today with a membership of around two hundred nationalities, and the numerous international organizations specializing in almost all areas of S&T and human endeavor, is an altogether new historical experience for mankind. It is proof of an emerging global pattern of human civilization built around nationalities of diverse traditions and cultural background. Marxian understanding of nationalities and Leninist assessment of imperialism had inspired national liberation movements of all continents, and played a major role in drafting the political map of the century.

Like the medieval Europe, India was a melting pot of races when, Western imperialism landed on its shores: The British had transformed the sub-continent into a prison of nationalities like the Tsarist Russia. Divide and rule was the official policy of the British, targeted to retard the natural development and renaissance of Indian nationalities: Their Bengal policy, leading to the ultimate division of Bengal, was possibly the worst of known examples. They divided India into territories, provinces and principalities in an arbitrary manner, cutting deep into the hearts and souls of the emerging Indian nationalities, in the name of administrative efficiency or political exigencies. Struggle for national independence simply rekindled the suppressed national sentiments and renaissance aspirations of the Indian people .

The struggle for national independence was transformed into a collective endeavor of diverse Indian nationalities, possibly, by Gandhi. Re-organization of states based on language or nationalities and a Union Republic based on federal constitution were the demands raised, mainly by the working class movement. Marxist-Leninist perceptions on nationalities as well as the Soviet Experience of uniting nationalities under a single state, had a profound influence on the re-organization of British India, after national liberation. Consolidating the ant—imperialist unity of Indian nationalities under a federal state structure or Union Republic, and at the same time ensuring their full and sustainable development, were seen by the Indian Left, as an inevitable historical necessity.

However, the bourgeoisie landlord classes, who were in a hurry to step into the shoes of British rulers, found no merit in such historic insights: The big bourgeoisie simply wanted to replace the British and rule the country either from Delhi or from Karachi, even by using the communal card, and the feudal kings were only keen to get back their petty fiefdoms. Indian as well as Pakistani constitutions, therefor, turned out to be happy compromises by their elite classes, who wished to continue in the footsteps of the British and hold the developing nationalities as their prisoners. India was declared a Union Republic in 1950, but it took more than six years of struggles and consultations for re-organizing the constituent states of the Union Republic, somewhat in line with the wishes and aspirations of Indian nationalities, and the process seems to be incomplete even today.

Indian Constitution is described variedly, federal as well as unitary, to suit the convenience of the elite classes. However, as it enters the fifth decade, most of its federal principles have simply evaporated into thin air: And, as feared by several among the constitution makers, status of member-states of the union republic is now reduced to that of municipalities; better said less on the municipalities and the so called local self government institutions (LSGIs), whose administrative capabilities and authority were reduced next to nothing, despite several constitution amendments and tall promises on Gandhian gram-swaraj, by the ruling classes (3).

There are hardly any signs of local or even national pride among the population: The elites of individual nationalities simply make hollow claims on their cultural heritage or achievements. Devoid of any real cultural content, our education system produces highly atomized, robot like half-humans and our men of letters look at language as a mere instrument for earning a livelihood, and not as a creative tool in the hands of the working people, for expressing and enriching their scientific and technological experience. Our elite classes have replaced Sanskrit with English as the new *vedabhasha* and they try to mystify scientific experience and declare it to be out of reach by languages spoken by common people. Even Hindi, the so called national language, possibly, is no exemption today (4). National renaissance and development of S&T were always an integral part of a total cultural experience of all peoples of the World: This was true of European countries, Japan, Russia, China, Korea, or Vietnam, and has to be for India as well. Nevertheless, following the footsteps of the British, India's ruling classes continue to block the flowering of its nationalities even today, and misuse even the constitution for this purpose.

Center-State relations as well as the division of responsibilities in the management of national economy were subjects of serious debates during the late seventies and early eighties, when CPI(M) led governments were elected to power in Kerala, West Bengal and Tripura. AKG Center for Studies and Research, Thiruvananthapuram, had organized a two day seminar on the subject in 1984 and this author had the privilege of presenting a paper on Center-State relations and hydro-power development in Kerala, in the context of the Silent Valley controversy (5).

Earlier in 1981, based on his working experience as the Member Secretary of the Kerala State Committee on S&T, he had presented a critique on *Center-State Relations and Science and S&T Administration in India* in a seminar organized by the Institution of Engineers (India) Cochin Center. Issues raised in that paper are even more relevant in the present context of the Central Government withdrawing itself from its patriotic responsibilities of development planning at the national level. This paper which had incidentally compared the Indian and Soviet systems of S&T Administration is reproduced below. (6).

Center-State Relations and the S&T Sector

India is a multinational country: Unity in diversity is often projected as the hall mark of Indian polity. But in the organization of administrative structures in our country, this is hardly recognized, S& T is no exemption. The British had organized S&T in the country, in a manner suited to their colonial objectives and perspectives. Structures like survey of India, geological, botanical or zoological surveys of India, Council for Scientific and Industrial Research (CSIR), and the like were created on the exigencies of colonial rule. Their organizational basis had little relevance to the realities of Indian polity and the requirements of a self reliant and self-sustaining type of developmental strategy, oriented to local needs and resources.

The three decades of independence had brought in no basic changes in this organizational set up. Even today, S&T organizations in the country are all oriented to "Delhi", and the bulk of S&T programs controlled from there. This dichotomy i.e. S&T being the near monopoly of the Central Government whereas the bulk of economic activities coming under the purview of State Governments, is a major inhibiting factor preventing our S&T developing a genuinely national character. The situation is hardly conducive to developing an S&T culture oriented to local needs and resources. The S&T administration in our country has to come out of its impersonal character and shed its imperial pretensions so as to identify itself with the life and culture of our people. Decision of the Central Government in early seventies to promote State Level S& T committee was an indirect recognition of this basic dichotomy in the S&T setup at the national. But the experience with the working of state level S&T Committees shows that this is no real solution. Such Committees are hardly any substitute for full fledged state level counterparts for DST,

If there were State level counterparts for CSIR, ICMR, ICAR and the like, they could have been affiliated or federated into the central bodies. Only a federal organizational structure can service S&T in the country on a professional footing and on a sustainable basis. Absence of such state level structures and the highly centralized unitary setup have led to the deterioration in the quality of state level engineering departments, technical and scientific education and national S&T capabilities in general. These apart, no worthwhile studies have taken place toward the identification and exploitation of the natural resources, at the state level. Even today, there exists no comprehensive compilation of our flora and fauna, no systematic studies and documentation on our climate, soil, water or mineral resources have been undertaken. In the recent past a few centers of excellence were created at the state level, in some of the States like Kerala.

But these institutions as well as the other technical institutions, research centers, universities and engineering departments at the state level have to evolve a well co-ordinated pattern of functioning, so that they serve the developmental needs of our people. Organizational structures and administrative mechanisms towards this have to be evolved and established. This can be achieved only through protracted debates among our professionals, their organizations, associations and S&T institutions in the state. It is obvious that the problems of S&T in Kerala are not confined to the state and call for solutions at the national level.

It will be of interest to study the organization of science and technology institutions in the erstwhile Soviet Union, which was a federation of autonomous republics of several nationalities. The Academy of Science of the US.S.R. had brought out in the late sixties, a commemorative publication to mark the golden jubilee of the formation of the Soviet Union. The organization of science in US.S.R. may very well be illustrated through a few quotations from this book. The Vice President of the US.S.R. Academy of Science had written: "Within the life time of a single generation, the people of some republics underwent a transition from a feudal society based on archaic agricultural systems to a socialist economy with a highly developed industry and mechanized agriculture. Peoples that did not even have a written language before the October revolution, now can boast of their own trained specialists. The children and grand children of peasants and nomads are designing and operating computers and other sophisticated equipments."

Boriservich, president of the Academy of Sciences of Byelorussian republic in his report on science in Byelorussia had stated: "The republic's council of ministers have set clearly defined tasks before the researchers working in the field of technical sciences to be completed during the current five-year period: To search for ways of improving automobiles, machine tools, agricultural machines, manufactured by the republic's industry, such as would provide at least 50 per cent increase in their overhaul period; to construct and introduce into Byelorussian production practice, a new apparatus for the drying and heat treatment of materials."

Academician Vekua, president of the Academy of Sciences of Georgian republic begin his report with the introductory commentary: "Georgian science has a glorious tradition reaching back to distant past." His report is flooded with the statements on the great achievements of Georgian chemistry, Georgian physics, Georgian mathematics, astronomy, agronomy and what not. Academician Abullayer, in his report on the science of the tiny republic of Azerbaijan talks of the recent developments in Azerbaijan cybernetics, developing of mathematical models for the directional drilling of oil wells for exploiting the rich oil resources of

Azerbaijan. Similarly, there are lengthy narrations on the achievements of the Ukrainian science, Lithuanian science, Moldavian science, Latvian science and the science in the Kirghiz: the republic of the Kirghizians who are one of the most ancient aboriginal people in central Asia.

It is not the intention here to prescribe any particular model for India's S&T administration. But the above account, as brought out by the spokesmen of the academies of sciences of former Soviet republics brings out the basic characteristics of Soviet science and its historical development. These are : (a) scientific research in Soviet Union was by and large organized as an integral part of social production, (b) S&T organization was highly decentralized but at the same time part of a well co—ordinated centralized system, and (c) Soviet Science was not impersonal in character but was well integrated into the overall socio-cultural life of various nationalities.

It is interesting to compare these with our own approach to Science and Technology and its development. For us science is universal and highly impersonal: to talk about 'Indian Science' is almost a taboo—smacks of national parochialism, to talk about the development of Manipuri Physics, Naga Chemistry, Carnatic Cybernetics or Assamese petrology or to suggest the formation of an autonomous Tamil or Kerala academy of sciences will almost amount to treason. We have come to believe that Science and Technology should be administered, funded and monitored by a strong Central Government from Delhi.

It has to be emphasized here that, be it agriculture, housing, roads, health, civic amenities, power, education or irrigation, each of these sectors have their specific regional and cultural characteristics. Each state is endowed with different types of natural resources and R&D efforts towards the identification and exploitation of these resources are best undertaken through state level efforts. Under Indian conditions, Science and Technology has to be highly decentralized not only because of its size and geographical diversity but also because of its cultural diversity.

The CSIR, ICMR, ICAR and other all-India institutions were formed after the British model, which had nothing much to do with Indian realities and contemporary aspirations of our people. It is possible that these organizations could have worked well on a federal principle with their autonomous State-level counterparts functioning under the State Governments. Instead, we see that individual institutions belonging to these central agencies are farmed out to different states on some consideration or other but mainly for appeasing public opinion in different states. The national laboratories and research institutions under these agencies have not succeeded in identifying themselves with the material and cultural life of local people of those regions, where theses institutions are located.

This defective approach can be seen even in the organization of voluntary professional associations and institutions. It is true that some of these organizations like the Institution of Engineers etc have their regional or state level chapters. But, by and large, they do not follow the natural division of the Indian Union into cultural and linguistic groups. The National Science Academy or the Indian Science Congress and other associations of scientists of individual disciplines can perceive of science only as an All India phenomenon. As a result, their overall impact on the life of our people and developmental policies has been minimal, if not negligible.

This sort of organizational dichotomy has poisoned even the value system among scientific communities. It is not the professional brilliance or professional contributions that make a good scientist, but one's position in the scientific bureaucracy. An Engineer or Scientist working at the state level institution or university is considered a smaller being compared to his Central counterpart. Often, we see Central level experts descending on the state level departments and institutions to render expert advice, not based on the strength of their professional standing or competence but just because they happen to be in Delhi, in the services of the Central Government: It is in noway different from the colonial value system, in which members of Royal Societies paid visits to inspect native institutions.

Science and technology institutions or voluntary professional associations in our country look up to Delhi for patronage, finance and facilities. Almost every one of them is directly or indirectly controlled and dictated on, in an ad-hoc manner, by the technocrats or bureau crafts sitting in Delhi. One fails to understand what sort of control, financial, administrative or professional, could be exercised from Delhi over a coconut research station situated in a remote village in Kerala or Tamilnadu.

If Indian science and Indian research has to be meaningful and relevant, it should come out of its impersonal character and shed its imperial pretensions. It should belong to where it is really needed, and where it is sought after. The future of Indian science and Indian research lies in the breaking up of the present highly centralized authoritarian structures, and erecting in its place a truly federal set-up, in tune with the spiritual, cultural, democratic and material aspirations of the people.

Lessons from past experience

The fact of disintegration of Soviet Union and the disappearance of socialist camp should not stand in the way of learning from the historical experience of organizing Soviet Science, and its greatly valued S&T cooperation with other countries, including the member countries of the Council for Mutual Economic Assistance (CMEA) (7). Soviet Union and the socialist camp could challenge and defend itself against the combined offensive and cold-war tactics of imperialist countries, for several decades, on the strength of its S&T.

Though internal subversion had demolished the Soviet State, the S&T institutions and industrial capacities created during socialist construction, have by and large survived, not only in the Russian Federation but also in the other constituent republics of the former USSR. Mutual cooperation among these institutions was rapidly re-established to a large extent under the framework of the Commonwealth of Independent States (CIS). Economies of the erstwhile Soviet Republics are once again getting integrated under this new dispensation. Working class politics in Russia as well as other CIS countries seems to be re-discovering and developing a new type of unity of diverse nationalities, on the strength of their common Soviet legacy, cherished by the vast majority of their working people.

Under Soviet Constitution, the Union Republics had exercised independent authority on all issues, outside the twelve items, mostly of international and inter-republican relevance and specified under article 73 of the constitution (8). The member republics directly participated in the governance of USSR as a whole, by their direct presence in the Supreme Soviet, the Presidium of the Supreme Soviet and the Government of the USSR: Chairmen of the Republican Soviets (ie. equal to speakers of our state legislative assemblies) were ex-officio Vice Chairmen of the Presidium of the Supreme Soviet, and Chairmen of Council of ministers of Republics (Chief Ministers) were ex-officio members of the Council of Ministers (Union Cabinet) of USSR. Institutions or State Committees for policy making as well as managing of deferent sectors of the national economy were constituted at the Union level based on federal principles as in the case of Academies of Sciences and S&T administration.

Soviet constitution had prescribed federal institutions, for ensuring the working together of governments in all sectors and at all possible levels. In sharp contrast, Indian constitution had packed the powers and responsibilities of state and center into three water tight compartments, central, state and concurrent lists, and then assigned all residuary powers to the Center. This was more like a partition deed, where as the Soviet Constitution laid down the ground rules for the mutual cooperation and working together of the Union and the Union Republics, with full autonomy and the right to secede granted to the republics. These were the objective reasons, why the dissolution of a mighty and immensely rich country like the USSR was a simple and exceptionally peaceful affair, and the reasons behind the slow and steady process towards reunion, despite the Russian Nazis and CIA interventionists. India could greatly benefit from this historical experience in rationalizing its Center-State relations, in the context of the dangerous distortions already brought in by the recent economic reforms and structural adjustments, enforced under the dictates of the global capital.

Power sector is one of the worst examples for these dangerous distortions which is blocking the smooth development of the national economy. Grid Power development was rightly included in the concurrent list by the constitution makers. But the new Electricity Act of 2003 is forcing the State Governments to dismantle the State Electricity Boards (SEB) set up under 1948 Act. Central Electricity Authority (CEA) and Regional Electricity Boards (REBs) had derived their federal authority and professional competence by coordinating the work of the autonomous SEBs, reporting to the state legislatures. This federal setup, developed after national independence, for the planned development based on self reliance, is being demolished or devalued for facilitating the entry of FDI and the authoritarian rule of a comprador bureaucracy sitting in Delhi that has assumed the responsibility for grid power development in the country, despite resistance put up by several member states. States will be mere agencies for realizing revenues by selling the electricity generated by large plants set up by monopoly capital at strategic locations divined by the Delhi bureaucracy (9).

Central public sector enterprises in the core sectors were products of the national five year plans and served as technology generators for the nation, through a process of national consensus in the inter-state council. Their shares were held by the President of India, on behalf all the Indian nationalities and the people of India. An impersonal Central Government had no political or moral right to sell the shares of these undertakings in the market and appropriate the sale proceeds for itself. But the senior bureaucrats in Delhi were doing this with impunity, without consulting even the Rjayasabha or Lokasabha. The Left parties have blocked the sale of shares of of BHEL and other Navaratna and Mini-Navaratna companies. Government of Jharkhand State had unsuccessfully resisted the sale of the mammoth BALCO Aluminum Plant but Tamilnadu had succeeded in blocking the privatization of the Neyveli Lignite Corporation (NIC).

It is becoming increasingly clear, that questions of management of Central Public Sector Enterprises, including their transfer of ownership or dissolution, cannot be and should not be left to the Central Government and its bureaucracy, simply because these enterprises were registered as per the company law for the sake of administrative convenience. Left parties, as well as, several among the regional parties were in the forefront of demands for a more equitable distribution of powers, between Center and States, including financial as well as policy making powers. But they seem to be silent on the patently unjust and one-sided moves of Central Government on the large core sector PSUs, which play a key role in the national economy, in the name of economic reforms and structural adjustments. True, the left had been critical about the reforms in general and had even successfully resisted the move for further dilution of government equity in BHEL and a few other public sector companies. But, it has not questioned the political and moral rights of Central Government to do this from a federal view point, nor was the arbitrary manner in which these extremely valuable federal assets were auctioned off. Opposition to this sell off was limited to a couple of corruption charges and empty parliamentary rhetoric by the left and the right. Faulty understandings, as well as the lack of appreciation of the rapidly changing class character of the Indian state were the root cause of these totally inadequate responses.

Indian State, led by the bourgeoisie-landlord classes, could for long years respond to the anti-imperialist sentiments of our people as well as the aspirations of our diverse nationalities for enriching their material and cultural life. National Five Year Plans, huge public sector initiatives with the help of the socialist camp and policies of national self-reliance, were seen by the people as the bulwark against imperialist exploitation and as bold initiatives by a strong and patriotic central government.

On the international scene India emerged as the natural leader of Non Aligned Movement (NAM), thanks to its success in building up a fairly strong indigenous technology base, and a vastly self-reliant national economy, compared to most other newly liberated countries. Patriotic professionals had dominated the elite classes during those years of anti-imperialist sentiments and even the militant Dravidian movements of early sixties were forced to mellow down their secessionist politics for fear of losing popular votes. Even the Left, with its largely objective prescriptions for Indian revolution, was forced to concede the patriotic and progressive content of Nehru-Indira regime. However, by mid eighties the discipline of national planning was substantially watered down, and with the collapse of the socialist camp a new regime has taken over the Central Government which is rapidly losing its patriotic credentials (10).

In collaboration with their foreign partners, the Indian big bourgeoisie has started building its shining empires, using the organizational expertise and manpower skills generated by giant public sector enterprises, which are being wantonly dismembered, destabilized or even demolished. The US initiative for nuclear cooperation, with the backing of Birlas, Ambanis and Tatas as well as their NRI supporters in USA, is a more recent, but typical example. As feared by the patriotic professionals within and outside of our nuclear establishment, this initiative was targeted at the destabilization of the Indian program for nuclear power development based on indigenous resources. The big bourgeoisie and their NRI supporters in USA were scheming to join the Global Nuclear Energy Partnership (GNEP), floated by USA at the expense of our own national program. National debate on this unpatriotic deal has exposed the real class character of the present Indian State.

The recent, but not yet concluded nuclear debate at the national level, had another side effect: It has opened up new avenues to fight against the authoritarian caucus and comprador bureaucracy that has taken over the central government establishment. Jayalalitha, Chairperson of AIDMK and the leader of opposition in Tamilnadu, has not only objected to the proposed Indo-US deal on patriotic grounds with sound technological arguments, but also raised the democratic demand that, all such international deals should get approved with two third majority in both houses of the Indian Parliament. However, it is to be noted that, center of gravity of India's nuclear power program presently lies within Tamilnadu territory, and the latest Russian offer for adding four more reactors at Koodankulam will substantially increase Tamilnadu's stake in the ongoing national program.

DMK being a member of the ruling UPA, Karunanidhi has not so far responded to this demand raised by his political adversary. However, Governor of Tamilnadu has made a strong plea for a thorough review of the center-state relations and rewriting of the Indian constitution in the interest of maintaining Indian unity. Such highly constructive initiatives by Dravidian politics need urgent follow up by the left forces and working class movement. This confirms also the need for enlarging the the scope of the debate on Center-State relations, beyond its traditional boundaries of public finance and the right to secede, and should cover the entire spectrum of statecraft and the working of the constitution (11)

Conclusion

There are lessons to be learned from the past experience of managing the different sectors of our national economy and a brief review of S&T administration had brought out several possibilities for innovations. Our Post and Telecoms departments have made rapid strides after their reorganization, taking the linguistic state as the administrative unit, even though a lot more could have been achieved by granting the P&T circles more autonomy and giving Indian Post and Telecom the genuine federal character it really deserved. Indian Railways could have responded to regional aspirations in a more rational manner far beyond the annual political circus staged by railway ministers, had it been re-organized into a federal entity after the national independence, instead of sticking to the arbitrary divisions of British days, in the name of administrative conveniences.

All India Radio, Doordarshan and Prasarbharathi could serve the cultural needs of various nationalities, if they are restructured on a federal basis. There is no logic, whatsoever, for not having TV channels and news broadcasting owned by State Governments, when BBC, CNN and others keep on brainwashing our people, 24 hours a day, 7 days a week. And, why not reconstitute the Kendra Sahithya Academy as an autonomous federal body, with the Chairmen of State level Academies as ex-officio members? These are just a few examples on how genuine federal practices could be grafted on to our administration.

Delhi regime had retained its imperial features and impersonal character, instead of drawing its strength and authority from its federal charecter. How the Indian President was dishonored on this republic day, by the Padmasree award for Sukumar Azhikod has to be an eye-opener for all: It is symbolic of the deep changes in the Indian polity (12).

The tendency to fabricate national consensus on issues and parade them as national policies without formally consulting the members of the Union Republic is on the increase, among the senior bureaucrats and central ministers.

Power sector reforms and the Electricity Act 2003 were forced on the country in this manner. Several such examples could be cited and the one related to minor ports is a recent example. Minor ports are in the concurrent list, and State Governments are their constitutional custodians. There was a recent national level consultation meeting on the subject at Kochi, organized by the Ministry of Surface Transport, but the concerned Kerala Minister came to know about this, only through newspaper reports. That is typical of the seriousness with which Central Government tries to evolve national consensus nowadays.

Meaningful consultations have become impossible even in the national Parliament, and its numerous consultative bodies are often maneuvered by the caucus of senior bureaucrats. Central Government is politically weak, today, and lacks in real federal authority. However, it has inherited, from the patriotic years of Nehru-Indira regime, immense administrative powers even outside the written constitution. Left is running a big political risk by neglecting these ground realities and in legitimizing the present Delhi regime with its parliamentary support. Policies and programs that emanate today from Delhi, related to vital sectors such as energy, power development, transport, telecommunications, IT, water management, irrigation, agriculture, education or health are not the product of our federal or democratic wisdom: They are mostly dictated on from outside, by the experts of imperialist countries, directly or indirectly through multilateral institutions, the English speaking elites among our bureaucrats and media men serving as agents and facilitators. This practice has to go. lock stock and barrel, and we should develop and nurture the institutions required for evolving the federal or collective wisdom of our nationalities and people at large.

Our constitution provides for an Interstate Council for facilitating federal consensus among the nationalities on issues of national import. Its constitutional role has been reduced to that of a ceremonial rubber stamp for approving the National Five Year Plan, drafted by the Planning Commission. Both the Sarkaria Commission and the National Committee to Review the Working of the Constitution (NCRWC) appointed by Vajpeye Governmnet had insisted on a more meaningful role for of this august body (13).

In the NCRWC report of 2002, its Chairman Justice MN Venkitachelliah had observed: *Article 263 had been most underutilized provisions of the Constitution. It can be imaginatively put into service by constituting subject or area specific Inter State Councils to deal with emerging new issues involving Union-State relations, more so in relation to areas touching upon international trade and participatory role therein of the States.* The report had recommended even a constitutional amendment for specifying the subjects for the functional Interstate Councils.

Servicing too many Interstate Councils may turnout to be cumbersome, considering the number as well as the variety of references that might be needed, when we move toward a genuinely federal administration as in the case the former Soviet Union. A more sensible approach will be to constitute as many *interstate councils or standing committees* as necessary for evolving federal consensus and to formalize their work. Even today, there are numerous informal consultations on several subjects but, they as a rule, are used for fabricating consensus and that is very typical of the fascist style governance. This has to give way to formal, open and mandatory consultations and that is the right way to checkmate the takeover of Delhi, by a coterie of comprador bureaucrats and politicians.

Notes:

1. A brave new world, based on technology was a vision shared by Marx and his contemporaries of humanist tradition: Shaw in *Back to Methuselah,* a brilliant science fiction piece and his last play, divines Man moving close to immortality through longevity achieved on the strength of technology and what he called as the theory of creative evolution. Azimov on the other hand permitted human society to expand into twenty five million worlds of diverse cultures, each world with four billion inhabitants. Technological pessimism and environmental fundamentalism were mainly a post-Marxian

phenomenon, products of the inevitable anarchy under Capitalism.

2. UN has a total membership of 184 nations; population of 57 nations was less than a million. The UN with its more than two dozen specialist organizations dealing with every aspect of human endeavor is a new historical experience for mankind, but mostly looked down by imperialists. This vastly democratic movement of nationalities is in fact seeking a new destiny for human race under the simple slogan of peaceful coexistence of diverse cultures or unity in diversity.

3. Local Self Government Institutions in India are possibly the least developed in the whole world: In USA, there were a total of 52 LSGI employees per 1000 population in the year 2002. Corresponding figure for India was only 2-see *Globalization and Downsizing of Governments,* paper by the author, published in the Passline of September 2005

4. Medium of instruction and language policy: Use of mother tongue as the medium of instruction at all levels and use of Indian languages in administration and by all branches of knowledge including S&T, were part of the cultural reforms promised by the national government. This has never materialized and India's elite classes have moved away from the concept neighborhood schooling, and continue to hold that language of S&T and even of the courts of justice has to be English.

5. Silent Valley Controversy: The proposal in 1978, for constructing a small hydro electric power plant (60 MW) was abandoned due to central intervention based on spurious environmental arguments. This was a major blow on the power development program of Kerala: As a result, close to two thirds of the hydro electric potential of the State remain untapped even today.

6. Author wrote this highly critical article in 1981 when he was the member secretary of the Kerala State Committee on Science and Technology. Those were years of intense debate on Center-State Relations among left intellectuals, because of the sharp ideological differences that existed between the Central Government and the Left ruled states.

7. Council for Mutual Economic Affairs (CEMA) served as the clearing house for the commercial relations and development plans of the countries belonging to the socialist camp. Higher level economic relations based on long term planning and dovetailing of S&T programs of member-nations were promoted by CMEA.

8. USSR Constitution: References made here are to the 1977 Constitution which claimed continuity of the earlier constitutions of 1918, 1924 (Lenin's time) and 1936 (Stalin's time)

9. A detailed analysis of the current situation in India's power sector was presented in a status paper presented by Engr. KR Umithan in the 22nd National Convention of Electrical Engineers, organized by the Institution of Engineers (India) held in Kochi on 24/25 th November 2006.

10. Several leading Marxist theoreticians, including Dr. Prabhat Patnaik and Dr. Ashok Mitra, have questioned the legitimacy of continuing the good old characterization of the Indian State by the mainstream left in the country, in the light of the ongoing reforms and their impact. A recent note by this author titled 'Ruling Elites plan for federal policing to defend Indian reforms' was published in the December issue of Red Star.

11. Indian state has developed and expanded considerably, in size as well as complexity, compared to the days of intense ideological polemics of sixties as well as the center-state

debates of early eighties. Right for self determination or right to secede was the main question discussed in the 1967 CPI(M) document, *Ideological Debate Summed Up,* prepared in response to the ideological challenges of Naxalite movement. Debates of early eighties were mostly centered on the practical difficulties of managing Left governments within the constitutional frame work, and the limited finances of State Governments. The framework for the debates on center-state relations has to be different today in the context of the changes in the class character of the Indian State and that of the Delhi regime.

12. Sukumar Azhikod a well known literary critic and social activist was conferred a Padmasri on the Republic day of 2007 which he openly declined to accept and people in Kerala had endorsed his refusal as one Man.

13. Left is silent today even on the Sarkaria commission, possibly because the Center is substantially weakened politically. But it refuses to see the vast administrative and financial prowess, the Center has acquired for itself, thorough the reform and restructuring process, eroding into the very spirit of our federal constitution. A politically weak Center wielding too much of administrative power, inherited from the past is an altogether unwelcome situation. The 2002 report and recommendations of NCRWC have taken serious note of these more recent developments. Surprisingly, these did not find even a mention in the 2004 Common Minimum Program of the Left and the UPA. However the Dravidian Parties have taken up the issues considered as a crucial for India's Peoples Democratic Revolution far more seriously than the Left, as may be judged from Jayalalitha's reaction to the Indo-US nuclear deal (see the Hindu of 23.12.2006) and the Tamilnadu Governor's address in the Legislative Assembly.

END

INDIAN AGRICULTURE: SEARCH FOR PATRIOTIC ALTERNATIVES

This is an essay in four parts, on the development of Indian agriculture. First part is a critical overview of the Vision 2030 document, recently presented by the Indian Council for Agricultural Research. Second part reviews the institutional responsibilities for the management of Indian agriculture, at various levels. The current status of agrarian relations and the emerging trends are briefly discussed in the third part. The fourth part quickly summarizes the search path for anti-imperialist and patriotic solutions. The paper was presented in the Asian agricultural conference held in Delhi, April 2012

1. Vision 2030 of ICAR

The Vision 2030 document, published in last January by ICAR (Indian Council for Agricultural Research—the apex R&D organization of India and founded in 1929 as Imperial Council for Agriculture Research), had summed up the present agricultural situation in the country, following words: "Our agriculture is dominated by small farmers, having small landholdings for cultivation. The average size of the landholding declined to 1.32 ha in 2000-01 from 2.30 ha in 1970-71, and absolute number of operational holdings increased from about 70 million to 121 million. If this trend continues, the average size of holding in India would be mere 0.68 ha in 2020, and would be further reduced to a low of 0.32 ha in 2030. This is a very complex and serious problem."

The document elaborates on the uphill tasks facing the planners: "A large number of smallholders have to move to post—harvest and non-farm activities to augment their income. The research focus should be to evolve technologies and management options to suit needs of smallholders' agriculture, and also to involve them in agri-supply chain through institutional innovations . . . . . To add to smallholders' problem, the quality of production environment is worsening. The problem of land-and-water degradation is becoming a key constraint in augmenting agricultural production. Available estimates reveal that nearly 120.72 million ha of land in the country is degraded due to soil erosion and about 8.4 million ha has soil salinity and water-logging problems. etc etc".

According to this ICAR estimates, nearly the entire currently cropped area in the country would be degraded by 2030 and the vision document goes on listing the other numerous problems to be tackled by S&T establishment in the country, for salvaging its dying agriculture. However, the document feels that "all these problems can be rectified by better management options . . . . The research and development challenge is to stop further degradation and go in for rehabilitation of degraded lands and water resources in a cost-effective manner. "

ICAR has been "co-coordinating, guiding and managing research, education and extension services in agriculture, including horticulture, fisheries and diary production in the country. There is a vast network with 97 ICAR institutes, 46 state agricultural universities, five deemed universities and one Central Agricultural University and 589 Krishi Vijgana Kendras (KVK) spread across the country." The vision document claims "to have played an enabling role in ushering green revolution and in the subsequent developments in agriculture in India through its research and technology development that enabled the country to increase production of food grains by 4-fold, horticultural crops by 6-fold, fish by 9-fold (marine 5-fold and inland 17-fold), milk by 6-fold, and eggs by 27-fold, since 1950-51; thus making a visible impact on national food and nutritional security."

It is customary to give credit to ICAR for India's green revolution, white revolution etc etc and it is also true that agricultural production in the country has been increasing steadily and in step with the population. Percapita production of food grains has been increasing, and India was free from hunger on the average, within a few decades of national independence. However, there are fears that, percapita production has already peaked some ten years ago, and there are concerns about the graph drooping further down. (Usta Patnaik.) And of course, several researchers had expressed serious doubts around the so called green revolution and the contributions made by ICAR and its all India network of institutions. These issues need detailed study, in the specific context of Indian agriculture continuing its primitive existence, despite tall claims by scientific communities and spokesmen of the establishment.

In fact, only a minuscule of the working people engaged in Indian agriculture (260 million) belong to the organized sector (1.5 million) and they mostly work for the plantations, dominated by the private corporate sector and big farmers. Vast majority of the working people, engaged in agriculture and allied activities, the self employed farmers as well as the agricultural labor, belong to the informal or unorganized sector of the national economy. Agricultural production has increased due to the expansion of cultivated land and increased productivity of land, thanks to expansion of irrigation facilities, use of chemical fertilizers, and switch over to high yielding variety seeds. Public investments in irrigation have played a key role in increasing production: There was an increase of over 30% in gross cropped area, thanks to irrigation even though the net cropped area had increased hardly by 12 % during the past sixty years. Gross irrigated area was only 17.4 % of cropped area in 1951-52 whereas the more recent figure is around 43 %. Assured water supply with the help of canal irrigation and tube-wells powered by highly subsidized grid electricity had facilitated not only application of chemical fertilizers but also adopting HYV crops.

The claims of ICAR over the green revolution were questioned, in the past, by several researchers. The more recent Report on Conditions of Work and Promotion of Livelihoods in the Unorganized Sector (August 2007) by the National Commission for Enterprises in the Unorganized Sector, under the Chairmanship of Arjun K Dasgupta should serve as an eyeopener in this regard. Quoted below are a few selected observations from Chapter-9 of this report, supported by extensive field studies:

- Nearly 60 percent of the farmer households have not accessed any source of information on modern technology. Among those who had accessed such information, the three main sources were other progressive farmers (16.7 %), input dealers (13.1 %) and radio (13 %).

- Government agencies such as Krishi Vigyan Kendra, extension workers, farmer visits, or even demonstrations and fairs have come to play a negligible role in disseminating information on modern technology.

- Both government and other sources were least accessed by the marginal and small farmers: As against 10 percent of the medium and large farmers, only around 4 percent of the sub-marginal and marginal farmers and 8 percent of the small farmers accessed information regarding improved practices and technology from extension workers.

- Quality and reliability of extension services appeared to be a major concern.

- Only 30 percent of the farmer households are members members of cooperative societies and of this one third did not make use of their services.

- At all India level, only 2 per cent of the farmer households were associated with organizations while 5 percent of them had at least one as a member of Self-Help Groups (SHGs). Such memberships are comparatively high in southern states and low in other states, surprisingly including West Bengal

The report had pointed out that, "rising cost of cultivation, low remunerations, high risks with frequent crop failures, declining agricultural growth, and mounting debts have all led the farmer to a distress like situation." It gives a graphic picture about the primitive nature of Indian agriculture and the hapless Indian farmer, "trapped by low literacy, lack of organization and poor connectivity with low levels of awareness regarding technology usage, institutional credit schemes and government's support initiatives." About 40 percent of farmer households dislike their occupation and farming, as an occupation, is looked down by the society as a whole. All these, including the rising suicide rates among farmers have, no doubt, everything to with the gross mismanagement of our agricultural sector.

2. Management of Indian Agriculture

An overview of the institutional responsibilities in the management of Indian agriculture, summarized as a chart, is given in the next page. Land being the most fundamental resource for agriculture, land use planning need to be seen as a crucial tool in managing agriculture development. This is so in any civilized country, but in India land is looked upon as a commodity, despite the town and country planning act being in existence for several decades. According to the act, village panchayats and town municipalities should have their own planning departments manned by trained personnel, and supervised by land use boards constituted by their respective local self governments. For over-viewing and guiding these activities and for making state level land use plans and production of quality maps, Land Use Boards were constituted by every member state of union republic.

Many of the State Land Use Boards are headed by junior or disgraced IAS officers and have turned totally dysfunctional with very little role clarity, and stagnating due to lack of working funds and professional manpower. Like the Kerala State Land Use Board, many of these organizations have taken up foreign consultancy assignments. Survey of India, initiated by the British, continues to be an imperial institution under the central government, and has not cared to develop its state level counterparts: Its linkages with State Land Use Boards are weak. Due to all these, India is extremely backward in the art and craft of cartography and the country simply does not possess even an essential minimum of inventory of quality maps, an essential input for the management of agriculture. All talks about national cropping plans etc based on the agro climatic resources of the subcontinent, make little practical sense, considering these grass-root level realities.

Situation with regard to water management and irrigation, as well as the weather resources, are similar to that of land use and land use planning. India is noted for its traditional canal irrigation networks, based on dams and reservoir as well as wells, tanks and bunds. Irrigation departments under the state governments are highly bureaucratized, and their linkages with agricultural departments, local administration and farmer collectives are extremely weak. Corrupt regimes at the state level naturally favor the rich peasantry, in the absence of comprehensive plans for individual river basins. Lack of professionalism in water resources planning and management has affected the quality and efficiency of the age old canal irrigation systems, leading to arbitrary increases in water-rates. There has been a massive shift to pumped irrigation, as a result: Cheap electricity, provided by State Electricity Boards, had led to even over-exploitation of ground water resources, all over the country. Central Water Commission, the federal custodian of our water resources has no counterparts at the state level, and as revealed in the recent Mullaperiyar conflict between Tamilnadu and Kerala, it is not even considered a competent body to arbitrate between two state governments.

Climate and weather studies in India are considered the sole prerogative of the Central Government. Daily, monthly and annual weather studies and forecasts by the Indian Meteorological Department (IMD) are made at regional levels and they have little relevance or use for the farming communities. In the absence of professional support from IMD, the farmers get guided by the local panchanga astrologers, or even water diviners. Our universities and research centers are engaged in climate studies related to global warming, sponsored by UNEP programs and foreign universities. They show little interest in weather and climate studies that are of relevance to local agriculture at the village or district level. Even the possibilities with our own weather satellites are not fully utilized. Rain gauges as well as weirs and notches, installed in the past for measuring surface water flows, have gone dysfunctional in many places, due to administrative neglect or lack of maintenance funds. Recently, IMD has drawn up plans for rectifying these deficiencies by strengthening itself. However, reconstitution and reorganization of IMD into a full-fledged federal body, so as to improve its coverage, quality, and efficacy, is not part of its immediate agenda.

MANAGEMENT OF INDIAN AGRICULTURE overview of institutional responsibilities				
Item	Central Government	State Governments	Local Self Governments	Farmer collectives
Land use plans	Low	Low	Nil	Nil
Water management	Mostly policy making	High	Nil	Nil
Weather forecasting	IMD—sole agency	Nil	Nil	Nil
Agricultural research	ICAR dominated	Low	Nil	Nil
Warehousing, price support	FCI, Central Warehousing	Low	Nil	Nil
Agricultural production	Policy making	Custodian of production	Nil	Nil
Human resource development	Nil	Nil	Nil	Nil
Development finance	Central plan +NABARD	State plans	Nil	Na
Overall	Bureaucratic regime.	Resource mismatch	Resource mismatch	No role

As indicated in the Vision 2030 document, 97 research institutes, 46 state agricultural universities, five deemed universities and one Central Agricultural University and 589 KVKs constitute the national network for agricultural research and extension services, presided over by ICAR. ICAR institutes cater to not only agricultural crops but also, horticulture, fisheries and animal husbandry and related technologies as well as mechanization. Like the Coconut Research Institute in my own village, their linkages with local farms and farming communities are extremely week.

There is an agricultural university in each state: They are autonomous bodies under the state government, but depend on ICAR for academic guidance as well as research funds.

Scientists working for ICAR, inevitably, develop a split loyalty due to the pulls and pressures of international, research dominated by global finance. In the absence of any coherent patriotic program for agricultural development, they look for global opportunities. Indian agricultural research continues to be weak and hapless, despite the long years of ICAR. It does not have roots in Indian farms and farming communities: We seems to believe that, even agricultural sciences has to be learned and taught only in English and not in Indian languages. We do not have books and literature in agricultural sciences in the languages spoken by our farmers and farm workers. And, that is reason enough to campaign for the restructuring of ICAR network on genuine federal lines and democratize its administration, in order to take it closer to the farming communities and the people at large.

Food Corporation of India was setup in 1964, in order to provide farmers with remunerative prices, to make food grains available at reasonable prices, and to maintain buffer stocks as a measure of food security. With its four zonal offices and over 35,000 employees FCI has turned a highly bureaucratic and inefficient set-up. Like all other Central Public Sector Undertakings, FCI has also failed to build up state level counterparts or subsidiaries, with sufficient autonomy to deal with region-specific and crop-specific problems, with the involvement of state governments and local self government institutions. There is another Central Warehousing Corporation (CWC), that have promoted State Warehousing Corporations as joint ventures with the state governments (50:50) with similar or over-lapping functions. CWC with its 17 regional centers and dealing in some 200 commodities look at export as its sole priority, and have no interest in the operations and management of its state-level subsidiaries, which have turned virtual orphans, without any worthwhile policy inputs or financial support from state as well as central governments. For effectively implementing the warehousing and price support strategies the organizational set up already created need to be streamlined and modernized.

State governments are looked upon as the custodian of agriculture production, and they are expected to perform, using the inputs provided by Central Government and its numerous agencies, over which they have very little control. Even here, policy making is seen as the sole prerogative of Central Government and its Planning Commission: even the National Development Council (NDC) is hardly consulted on policy questions on agriculture. Agricultural Prices Commission finds even questions related to terms of trade difficult to handle, due to numerous regulatory complexities and diverse tax regimes. Liberalization of trade and bilateral trade agreements has brought in further complications in policy management at the state level.

Despite constitutional provisions for decentralized administration, several related sectors like social forestry, minor irrigation, local transport, small and village industries etc continue to be outside the purview of local governance. As already pointed out, Indian farmers are poorly organized as a collective and play virtually no role, or play an extremely weak role in policy making, related to land use, water resources management and irrigation, crop development, mechanization, or even formulating development plans.

Even states like West Bengal and Kerala where land reforms and democratic decentralization of administration has registered substantive progress, farmers and their collectives play little role in the management of agriculture. A recent (January 2009) report by the West Bengal State Commission on Agriculture had lamented on the lack of participation by farmers and their collectives in the formulation and implementation of farm development programs in that state. If that is the situation in a state like West Bengal, the over all situation in the country must be far far worse.

3. Managing the uneven development

Developments in agrarian relations in the country have been extremely uneven. Peasants' struggle for land has succeeded in some measure during the six decades of national independence. Land reforms were attempted in almost all Indian states, and under influence of the left, the reforms were seriously pursued in Kerala, West Bengal and Tripura, where the democratic movement got considerably strengthened. Kerala has experienced a big shift from food crops to cash crops, typical of capitalist agriculture. Farm incomes per unit area cultivated as well as per person engaged in agriculture are nearly three times the national average, in Kerala. There are two agricultural workers per cultivator in Kerala if we go by the census counts, and the ratio is just the reverse for the country as a whole. Agriculture workers as well as the entire informal sector workers in Kerala command much higher wages and better working conditions compared to their counter parts elsewhere in the countries.

The shift from sustenance agriculture based on food crops to capitalist agriculture based on cash crops is taking place all over the country, slowly but steadily, and the intervention programs designed by the Delhi bureaucracy with minimal or ineffective consultations at the lower levels, including the farmers' collectives, have proved, by and large, ineffective. There is a crisis situation emerging, and the Central Government and its policy makers are using the opportunity to plan a total surrender of the agricultural sector to global capital. Technology developments like genetically modified crops and micro climate controlled agriculture and others are opening up totally new horizons in agriculture. And the emerging trends are uneven, unbalanced and unsustainable in the long run. They need to be carefully analyzed and clearly understood if we are to decide on a strategy for countering these new imperialist offensives.

VK Ramakrishnan, the noted agricultural economist reviewed the current status of Indian agriculture in an article published in the last issue of Marxist (Jan-June 2011): This article, based on an extensive study of several Indian villages had observed: "India is a vast and living example of the rule that capitalism penetrates agriculture and rural society in a myriad ways. If the development of capitalist relations in agriculture is clearly the major trend, it is equally clear that agrarian relations are marked by national, regional and local diversity, and by extreme unevenness in the development of capitalist relations of production and exchange . . . . Variations in agrarian relations are not just a matter of differences in the level of development of the productive forces leading to some regions being more or less 'capitalist' than others; the crucial feature of capitalist development in agriculture is, as Lenin wrote, that 'infinitely diverse combinations of this or that type of capitalist evolution are possible.' If this formulation was true of old Russia (or old China), it is true too of India, where the material forces constituted by backward ideologies of hierarchy and status add immensely to the 'peculiar and complex problems' arising from spatial diversity . . . . Data from nine villages in the States mentioned above showed that 21 per cent of households (mainly poor peasants) actually had negative crop incomes. By contrast, the average agricultural income of households in the top docile was over 3.2 lakhs per household. Not only do the data show that aggregate incomes from agriculture are highly unequal across cultivator households, they also show that there are large variations in the costs of cultivation and profitability across crops, and, for a given crop, across regions. Variations in the profitability of crops across different classes are substantial . . . .

. . . . Data shows differences in gross output and net annual incomes from agriculture per acre of operational holding across villages and between cultivators operating smallest twenty and largest twenty land holdings. The data show that, given the concentration of land and other means of production in their hands, landlords and rich peasants are able to keep production costs lower than middle and poor peasants. In contrast, the poor peasants are forced to buy inputs at a higher unit price than the rich, and to pay rents for land and machinery. With more efficient input use, and better access to markets, landlords, big capitalist farmers and rich peasants also receive a higher income per unit of production than middle and poor peasants."

True, India is a subcontinent of diverse cultures and subcultures, supported by vastly different agro-climatic conditions. Politically, we are a conglomeration of numerous developing nationalities and call ourselves a multinational country. The process of nationality development in the sub-continent was frozen by the British in their imperial interests, and the ruling classes, that inherited political power from the colonial rulers, were in no mood to complete the unfinished tasks of national liberation. Even the re-organization of Indian states on linguistic or cultural lines, a legitimate dream of Indian independence movement, was resisted by them. Indian big bourgeoisie and our ruling elites sustain their hegemony over the Indian people with the help of neocolonialists, and by blocking and suppressing their struggles for cultural and material development.

Our elite classes have even invented even jargons like Unity in Diversity, for seeking moral justifications for the oppressive development policies, pursued by the Indian State. Culture is not generated in a vacuum: It springs from the material life of people. It is sustained by science and technology, and culture is the product of autonomous development of a society, with its own personality, history and geography. The abstract universal man is pure invention by the intellectual classes and doe not exist for the vast majority of the working people of our century. We have seen, in the earlier sections, the bogus character and hollow claims of the inefficient agricultural development programs followed by the Indian state, with little or no involvement of our farmers and their collectives, as well as the people at large. Vision 2030 of ICAR is a sure recipe for the further alienation of our working people from the Indian State, that rules over them. It will end up as an even bigger failure than the earlier development program, which has virtually pushed Indian agriculture into the present chaotic situation. And it could be salvaged only through the prolonged political struggles of the working people, and vast majority of them belong to agriculture.

4. In conclusion:

Indian agriculture continues to be primitive in terms of technology and organization, even after six decades of intervention by the Indian state under the leadership ICAR. However, it has already entered the capitalist phase of development which is uneven, unstable and unsustainable. Vision 2030 document prepared by ICAR is incompetent to address the emerging crisis. Central Government and the elite classes that rule the country are getting ready to hand over the agriculture sector to foreign monopoly capital under the pretext of solving an impending crisis.

The big capitalist farmers and rich peasants are sure to join hands with the foreign monopolists in this process of takeover, as part of the ongoing globalization process. This will be at the cost of the rest of the farming community, consisting of small and marginal farmers, agricultural workers and other sections of our rural proletarians.

This process is sure to be prolonged and protracted. The big capital is equipped with modern farming technologies and agricultural research organized by imperialist states. A well planned strategy and effective intervention by the Indian state are absolutely necessary for protecting the interest of the farming communities and the country at large. ICAR and other central government organizations need to be strengthened by developing their state level counterparts and then transforming them into genuine federal institutions, capable of defending national interests.

Rural proletarians of India's informal sector, including the agricultural workers need to be unionized for fighting for their basic human rights, such as minimum wages, reasonable working conditions, and social security. The report on unorganized sector by Arjun Sengupta committee on the unorganized sector of the national economy has highlighted the need as well as the possibilities for regulating the labor market in the informal sector.

In fact, Arjun Sengupta report is the byproduct and legacy of the decades long struggles waged by the informal sector workers, in several parts of the country, under the leadership of working class parties which has by now acquired adequate strength and expertise to formulate and campaign for an alternative agriculture development program that is truly patriotic and anti-imperialist.

END

LANGUAGE POLICY AND INCLUSIVE DEVELOPMENT*

Even after six decades of independence English dominates Indian administration: It is the medium of higher learning in Indian universities and the language of Indian science and technology. Major contributor to exclusive development, in the past, was the language policy, practiced by Indian State. Discussions on inclusive development make little sense, outside the frame of our language policies.

Look at our agrarian sector: Literature on our crops, soil or climate is simply not available in the languages spoken by our farmers and farm workers, numbering around 180 million: Kerala is the land of coconuts, but there is no scientific literature in Malayalam dealing with the tree, its cultivation, products and related technologies. Agricultural universities of India and ICAR institutions speak only English, have little contact with our farming communities and mostly work for publishing papers in foreign journals.

We have around 45 million industrial workers, including the ten million in organized sector: spinners, weavers, welders, blacksmiths, fitters, electricians, plant operators, telephone workers, auto drivers, motor mechanics etc. They would love to read technical literature on their trades, in their mother tongues; for improving skills, efficiency and quality. That sort of literature, including safety manuals, hardly exists in Indian languages.

We have a large army of construction workers: masons, bricklayers, bar-benders, form workers, painters, carpenters, plumbers, electricians, lift and crane operators, loading and unloading workers, and then the so called attimari or head load workers. Nobody knows, from where they come, how they get trained, and where they disappear: They hardly get any formal training in their trades, though their share in GDP continues to expand, every year.

Specifications and standards for public works are prepared and published in English. If published in local languages, they could impart technical knowledge to millions of construction workers, contractors and engineering students, and bring in transparency in our public works. Indian Standards prepared by BIS, at huge cost to public exchequer, will help in educating workers and using their creativity, if published in local languages.

In the health sector, doctors, nurses and other paramedical staff learn their trade only in English. Medical prescriptions and instructions are made out only in English. Indian languages stand virtually banned by the ICMR and Indian medical profession. Even Ayurveda has turned English, despite its claims on holy origin. Ayurveda is learned and taught in English, nowadays, though the original texts were written in Indian languages.

Best way to develop the capabilities of our languages is to start using them for learning and teaching science and technology. This will, not only galvanize the learning process but also lead to the creation of a vibrant indigenous S&T. This, in turn will help the working people to participate in technological and scientific innovations**. This is the lesson to learn from developed countries, and also developing nations like Korea, Vietnam or China.

English speaking intelligentsia is a key constituent of our elite classes that rule our country. Language policy, now practiced by Indian state, immensely suits their selfish interests: First, it helps them to sustain their hegemony over the working people, as in the good old days of Brahmin domination, when Sanskrit was the *veda bhasha and deva bhasha* and holding the same status as Latin in medieval Europe. And secondly, it helps them to migrate to the West, and extract global prices for their labor power.

This microscopic section of our society insists that knowledge in general and S&T in particular has to be taught and learned only in an imperial language, if the country is to benefit from modern technologies. Such hypotheses by the elite classes of Europe were demolished by the industrial revolution and Latin replaced by Portuguese, Spanish, English, French, Russian or German. And, the socialist revolutions, that followed the two global wars, led to an even bigger upheavals in the language policies of nations-states and nationalities.

Our language policy is blocking the creativity of a billion people: Stagnation and exclusive growth are the inevitable results, as evidenced by our poor performance in innovations and inventions. Deliberations on inclusive development, outside the framework of national language policy, are typical of the hypocrisy practiced by our English speaking intelligentsia.

---

* Presented in the seminar on Inclusive Development organised by CUSAT and E Balalanndan Research Foundation in June 2011

INVENTIONS AND INNOVATIONS IN INDIA: THE BLEAK PICTURE*

India is the second populous country, next only to China. It is well known that, India's medal tally in Olympics or Asiad is hardly commensurate with its population size: China had cornered maximum number of medals in the last Olympics where as India's rank was as low as fifty. With regard to the share in scientific inventions and technical innovations also, India lags behind even smaller countries, if we go by the statistics related to patenting activities reported by the World Intellectual Property Organization (WIPO-http://www.wipo.int)

Table below summarizes the information on population and patenting statistics for selected countries for the year—2005/2006. Korean Republic, with hardly five percent of Indian population, had more than 166,189 patent applications compared to India's 24, 505 in the year 2006. Chinese population was nearly 25 times more inventive compared to population, if we go by patent statistics with regard to new inventions and patenting activities. Based GDP basis Chinese economy was nearly 12 times more innovative compared to Indian economy, if we go by the number of patent applications filed per billion dollar of GDP on a PPP basis. The table brings out the extreme backwardness of India's inventing communities compared to those of the developed as well as developing countries.

Country	Population Million	No of Patents filed	Patents Per Billion $ GDP	Patents Per Million Popln
India	1095	24,505	2	4
China	1305	210,501	24	93
Korea	48	166,189	122	2591
USA	296	425,966	20	742
Japan	126	408,674	87	2720
Germany	82	60,585	19	583
UK	60	25,745	10	290
Russia	143	37,691	33	196

TABLE: PATENT STATISTICS IN INDIA AND OTHER SELECTED COUNTRIES-YEAR 2006

The abstract statistics given in tabular form are in harmony with real-life experience, as well. Industrially developed countries like USA, UK, Japan, Korea and Russia continue to be the leaders in innovative activities. China has caught up with them in a big way, in recent years, and in terms of patent registration per unit of population as well as unit GDP, China is far ahead of India and is fast catching up with the more developed countries with regard to number of patent registration per year. Global markets are getting flooded with highly innovative Chinese goods: consumer and consumer-durable as well as High-Tech capital goods. A decade ago Indian markets were flooded with cheap low quality CFL lamps, at one tenth the prices offered by Philips, GE and other global corporates: Now good quality Chinese CFL is available at half the market prices, in select shops and importers in Kochi.

Cheap LED technologies for energy efficient lighting are now rapidly developing in China: Such products have become suddenly popular even in the Broadway retail shops of Kochi. In the recent International Exhibition in Delhi on non-renewable energy, organized by GOI, Solar PV industry of China was the star performer: They were offering technology and whole range production lines for the mass manufacture of Solar PV panels. Global toy markets are flooded with highly innovative Chinese toys. And then in thermal and hydro power plants, China is offering stiff competition to BHEL, on its home ground. In shipbuilding, China has emerged a world leader. Lenova and Howai type initiatives, by China's public sector R&D institutions, have simply transformed the global markets for IT and communications.

Most of the less complex light engineering goods of China, like electronic gadgets, toys, medical electronics etc, are developed by worker-innovators, manufactured by small enterprises, and then marketed by giant global trading organizations in the public sector. Unlike India, China has a large army of innovators amongst its lay working people, who has easy access to the global markets and modern technologies. Patents, national standards, design drawings, technology sheets etc etc are available in Chinese languages. Unlike in India, one need not be an academic or proficient in English for accessing S&T, which is taught and learnt in the native languages of China.

Scientists, engineers, management experts, administrators and other professional classes in India seems to believe that University or Higher Education in general, and professional education in particular has to be taught and learnt only in English. There are hardly any good textbooks in Indian languages, for teaching and learning science, technology or management. Institution of Engineers (India), Indian Medical Association, Institution of Chartered Accountants, Management Associations and other professional bodies refuse to speak in vernacular: Their journals, as a rule, are published only in English. No worthwhile S&T literature exists in Indian languages.

O&M manuals of equipment sold in the country are generally in English language. Even our drugs and pharmaceutical laws do not compel drug manufacturers to provide essential information in the language of the drug users. PWD Standards and specifications that should guide the construction and maintenance of public works in different regions are produced and published only in English, and not in the local languages. National Standards serve as an extremely effective instrument for dissemination of valuable S&T information: However, our Bureau of Indian Standards (BIS) speaks only English and a little bit of Hindi, sometimes: BIS does not even recognize the massive market potential for the tens of thousands of national standards, if they could be published in Indian languages.

Intelligentsia and elite classes of our country have a deep rooted vested interest, in the continuation of English as the medium of higher education as well as the language of S&T in the country even after six decades of national independence, in addition to serving as the virtual official language of the union republic. The situation serves their selfish interests two counts: First, it provides them with global mobility and plenty of value to their skills in the international market. Secondly, it helps them to perpetuate their hegemony over the rest of society, as in the good old days, when Sanskrit was considered as Veda Bhasha as well as Deva Bhasha.

In feudal Europe, Latin had played the role of Sanskrit in India. As industrial revolution swept over Europe, Latin was replaced by modern European languages like English, French, Italian, Spanish or Portuguese, as the language of S&T as well as the medium of higher education in Universities. This was European renaissance, when literacy was rendered universal and compulsory, and the entire mass of working people got exposed to the brave new world of Science and Technology. Working people turned inventors and innovators in their thousands, in every European country. Inventions like steam locomotive, flying machines, bicycle, telegraph, telephone, electric lamps, clock towers pumps and power stations were mostly the creative contributions by craftsmen and journeymen and not of academics of Royal Societies.

The numerous Eurasian nationalities, small and big, under the Czar of Russian Empire, started using their own mother tongues as the language of S&T and the medium for higher education soon after their liberation, and set up their own Republican Universities under the Soviet regime. The present-day CIS countries, from Ukraine to Azerbaijan and Mongolia, have academic and research institutions, today, comparable to the best in our own country, and their societies are far more innovative, if we go by WIPO Statistics. The data reveals frightening backwardness of India with regard to creative innovations of our people on one hand and the national economy on the other. This is a self aggravating defect and need urgent correction.

---

*   Published in Passline April, 2011

POWER SITUATION WORSENS, GOVERNMENT LOOKS HELPLESS*

Collapse of Northern, Eastern and Western power grids, a few months ago, was big news even on BBC. Many US newspapers ran catchy headlines on the perennial failures of Indian government in meeting power sector targets. Demands for further deepening of reforms were echoed by sections of Indian bourgeoisie. Sam Petroda, adviser to Government on infrastructure, sounded more than sober: In his view grid collapses and blackouts are not unusual even in USA. However, the fact is that, our power sector suffers from serious shortcomings. They are worsening by the day, and a sort of policy vacuum has set in, as the World Bank initiated reforms enters its third decade.

As a concurrent subject, electricity was included in the seventh schedule of Indian Constitution: Indian Electricity Act 1948, like many other statutes inherited from British days, had a federal character. State Electricity Boards (SEBs) were conceived as the custodian of electric power grids at the state level, and a Central Electricity Authority (CEA) was conceived as a federal entity: Its members were nominated by the President of the Union Republic. Five Regional Electricity Boards were set up, later, functioning under CEA supervision in order to ensure better cooperation among neighboring states in the operation of power systems, as well as their planning and standardization.

The 1948 Act was flexible enough to accommodate large investments as in Neyveli Lignite Corporation and Damodar Valley Corporation by central government, private sector power plants like Tata Power of Mumbai or Calcutta Electric Supply Undertaking, in private corporate sector. Later the National Thermal Power Corporation (NTPC) was setup for facilitating super thermal power stations at the mine-heads and taking power to population centers far off from coal mines, using high voltage transmission network. National Hydel Power Corporation (NHPC) and National Power Grid Corporation (NPGC) were the natural corollaries of these successful initiatives by central government at the national level.

Policy making powers remained entirely with Central Government, but administration of power sector was fairly decentralized. State governments and their SEBs had a say in the management of state and regional grids and the development of regional and national grids, thanks to the CEA, which had functioned as a federal authority from the very beginning. However, it was virtually impossible for state governments to exercise the autonomy granted to them, because of the discipline of central planning and financial dependencies on central government. Discipline of national five year plans had its obvious relevance in a developing economy: Per-capita annual electricity consumption in India was a meager 25 KWH per year at the time of independence, and to increase it to a decent level of few thousand KWH, as in developed societies, demanded extensive coordination with other sectors of the national economy, like coal mining, oil and gas production, transportation, rail and road development etc.

National five year plans had several other advantages as well: technology development at the national level leading to a high level of self reliance with regard to the manufacture of generation-transmission equipment, a rational fuel policy with regard to the choice of primary energy viz a viz coal, oil, gas, atomic, solar, hydel and other renewables and also human resources development. India could achieve quickly, a fairly high level of standardization of power systems, equipment designs, processes and practices essential for orderly development. Despite frequent policy interventions by World Bank and pressures from foreign collaborators, national enterprises like BHEL and others achieved a high level of technological competence. By the early nineties, when World Bank started insisting on implementing its reform package, India's power sector had already recorded achievements that were comparatively far ahead of the rest of the national economy.

Per capita electricity generation and consumption in the country had increased by sixteen times, during the forty year period 1950-1990, when per capita GDP had only hardly doubled. Over 75,000 MW of capacity was added to Indian power grid, during this period. Most of the equipment and systems for this massive capacity expansion were designed and manufactured within the country; not a small achievement for a developing nation like India. Some nine million farmers were given free or highly subsidized electricity, a key input for the so called green revolution.

Two million small scale industries and 45 million households were provided with electricity. The country had built up the capacity for manufacturing and installing some 5000 MW of power, every year, which could have been doubled or even trebled, in ten years time, within the framework of appropriate policy packages. According to a World Bank appraisal in early nineties, electricity was priced in India at half to one third of the then prevailing international prices; revenue gaps of all the SEBs in the country taken together was only about 20 percent, despite the low level of price realization.

These were no mean achievements; however the financial position of SEBs were worsening by the day, due to the persistent revenue gaps, and the sector suffered from a never ending financial crisis. Quality of supply was deteriorating and there were too many planned and unplanned outages, and capacity shortages were perennial due to a variety of reasons. An increase of 25 to 30 percent in the average tariff of SEBs could have generated massive funds for re-investing and capacity addition, and the badly needed system improvements. Political leadership was reluctant to enhance the tariff for bridging the revenue gaps of SEBs, and planners refused to increase the share of plan funds for the power sector. In the name of improving the financial discipline of SEBs, Power Finance Corporation (PFC) was floated in 1986 for augmenting funds for the rehabilitation plans of SEBs, drafted by CEA.

Plans for the standardization of power plants were launched by CEA, using indigenous equipment in order to bring down investment and running costs of power plants, with the cooperation of indigenous equipment manufactures as well as consulting organizations in the power sector. Equipment manufacturers like BHEL launched numerous R&D programs for the better and more efficient utilization of Indian coals, the principal source for power generation in the country. None of these innovative projects, including the programs for enhancing the manufacturing capacities for power plant equipment, had attracted support of World Bank and the Indian planners, who had turned increasingly comprador, under the rising influence of a new globalization drive.

World Bank advisers were keen to utilize the so called investment crisis for the opening up of India's power sector to FDI. Indian market for power equipment and systems was massive: The extremely low electricity consumption level of a billion people was seen by the developed countries as a massive opportunity for exporting power equipment and related services. Policy initiatives by World Bank, in the early nineties had a two-fold objective: Force-opening of the Indian market for power equipment was the first, and destabilizing the indigenous technological capabilities and institutional framework, built after national independence was the second, and possibly even more fundamental.

Department of power was part of the Ministry of Energy of GOI for long: An independent Ministry of Power started functioning with effect from 2nd July 1992, and was asked to overview the implementation of World Bank recommendations on power development. CEA, the federal authority, constituted as per the1948 Act, was totally bypassed and its functions virtually taken over by the new Department of Power, under the pretext of solving the so called investment crisis in power sector. Though electricity was in the concurrent list, this new central ministry was de'facto given the exclusive charge of "perspective planning, policy formulation, processing of projects for investment decision, monitoring of the implementation of power projects, training and manpower development and the administration and enactment of legislation in regard to thermal, hydro power generation, transmission and distribution in the country." Electricity Act 1948 was given a silent burial, and later replaced by a new act, without the formal consent of state governments and state legislatures.

The new act administered by the department of power has virtually transformed grid power development and its administration as the near exclusive territory of the central bureaucracy. SEBs who served as the custodian of power development in their respective states were directed to un-bundle themselves into separate companies in charge of generation, transmission and distribution. Power grids are normally conceived, built and operated as natural monopolies, and it is impossible to build and operate them as public utilities without a competent political custodian. A power grid can operate only within a given geographical and political boundary. Even these fundamental aspects were overlooked by our reform enthusiasts and as a result, state governments found it near impossible to implement the un-bundling stipulations of the new act.

Three states Kerala, Bihar and Jharkhand have not implemented the unbundling instructions of the 2003 Act, even today. The fifteen states that have implemented them in some form or other, mainly for the sake of conformity, have not benefited in any manner. States like Odisha and Delhi, the early birds of un-bundling reforms are, reportedly, the worst sufferers today. Despite the ushering in of Regulatory Commissions at the state and central levels, revenue gaps persist in their operations: financial crisis continue to cripple almost every distribution utility in the country. The recent nine member high-level committee appointed by Planning

Commission for reviewing the un-bundling scheme has concluded that, it has not delivered the desired results.

Implementation of the 2003 Act has drastically weakened electricity administration in the country, at the state, regional and central levels; organizationally as well as professionally. The eighteen State Electricity Boards in the major states and the electricity departments in the half a dozen minor states and the five Regional Electricity Boards, together with their half a million skilled workers and engineers, had served as the depository of knowledge and experience, related to power grid operations and grid power technologies in the country. CEA, as a federal authority provided the essential linkages between central and state governments as well as the numerous enterprises and institutions under them. The role played by CEA and the spectrum of professional services rendered by it was similar to that of the Central Electricity Generation Board (CEGB) of Britain.

Working in tandem with equipment manufacturers as well as consultancy organizations in the country, in public as well as private sector, CEA served as a truly federal body, in support of our power system utilities. During the early years of power development in independent India, it had played a key role in the design of power plants and transmission distribution systems. Later, the role was changed to that of an apex level consultancy organization for feasibility studies, design reviews for power plants and systems, performance evaluation and reporting, standardization of design, and human resources development. The 1992 reform was primarily aimed at the destabilization of CEA and the breaking up its organic linkages with the power utilities.

CEA was not taken into confidence in 1992, when the ministry of power decided to promote FDI in a big way, under the so called fast-track route that had assured super-profits to foreign investors. State Governments and their SEBs were asked to sign up long term contracts for buying electricity from them, on a cost plus basis. There was a scramble for the no-risk investment opportunities offered by the fast-track scheme. However, with the scam around Dhabol power project of Enron getting nation-wide attention, the fast-track scheme was dropped like hot potatoes. TU movement in Mumbai had taken the Enron issue to Mumbai High Court, much before it had turned a national scandal, but the learned judges were not impressed by such working class initiatives.

Despite the Enron debacle, Ministry of Power as well as the DOP bureaucrats in Delhi pressed on with the power sector reforms, by proposing a new electricity statute. Old-timers of CEA and other patriotic professionals had expressed their apprehensions about the reforms and also recorded their dissent on Electricity Bill-2000, in the numerous seminars, organized in Delhi, Kolkota, Mumbai, Banglore and other places. According to them, the1948 Act was broad enough to accept private sector initiatives, if found necessary and there was no need for the new statute: The real problem was, in their opinion, lack of political will to implement the provisions of the existing act, in letter and in spirit, especially those provisions related to tariffs.

The proposed act was adversely commented on, even by professional bodies like the Institution of Engineers (India). However, the Ministry of Power continued its public campaign for the new statute, using the muscle power of PSUs under it: the NTPC, NGPC and PFC. The bill was finally enacted by the Indian Parliament in 2003. The new act sealed the fate of CEA, by transforming it into a mere "attached office" of DOP: its responsibilities are now confined to compiling and publishing of power sector statistics. And, as a rule, SEBs ceased to function as the custodians for power development in the states and Regional Electricity Boards were disbanded.

Under the new policy environment, PFC with employee strength of less than 300 has turned the kingpin of power sector development in the country. This lean organization has a closely held board, which is dominated by the so called independent directors, with very little exposure to the development of national power sector. Though rehabilitation of SEBs was its primary founding objective, PFC investments are, nowadays, mostly in green field projects: Ultra Mega Power Projects (UMPP) based on the controversial super critical technology were promoted and financed by PFC. Apart from the Special Purpose Vehicles created for the 12 UMPPs and the six wholly owned subsidiaries like PFC Consulting Ltd, it has also promoted several joint ventures, such as Coastal Karnataka Power Limited, Coastal Tamil Nadu Power Limited, Coastal Maharashtra Power Limited, Orissa Integrated Power Limited, Jharkhand Integrated Power Limited and Akaltara Power Limited.

Over the past one decade, net-worth of PFC has increased several fold: With an equity base of Rs.1148 Crore, its accumulated profit was well over Rs.18,000 Crores as on March 2012. Its profits have increased nearly four times during the decade, to more than Rs.3500 Crore in 2011-12. Its annual business income has more than doubled to Rs.13,037 Crore during the last four years. PFC is now the flag ship company of DOP and it is entrusted, with responsibilities, that are far beyond its professional competence.

In March 2008, PFC had established the PFC Consultancy Ltd (PFCCL), as its subsidiary, for providing consultancy services to the power sector, on the strength of serving the state power utilities, its captive clientèle, for nearly two decades. This subsidiary, with its skeleton staff of about a dozen or two, has made a profit close to Rs.120 Crore, within the short span of last three years. Subsidiaries, joint ventures and special purpose vehicles, sponsored by corrupt bureaucrats are the breeding grounds of crony capitalism. Just a few days ago, PFCCL has issued "a global invitation for expression of interest for a joint venture partner in power sector consultancy". The invitation is open up to 31st August: Possibly the Ministry of Power has already shortlisted the parties to be invited.

Electricity Act—2003 is firmly in position now for nearly a decades and the PFC and PFCCL were making massive profits. But the state power supply utilities continue to incur heavy financial losses, even today. According to the latest all India report, complied and published by PFC, financial losses incurred by all the state power utilities together was around Rs.34, 000 Crore in 2010-11. And, this was around 20 percent of their total revenue for the year, and the revenue gap was of the same order as in 1992, when India had embarked on its World Bank dictated reforms.

The country is worse off now, compared to the days, when the reforms were pushed down the unwilling throats of state governments. Power utilities at the state level have frittered away their organizational resources, thanks to the highly destructive un-bundling exercises. A feeling of total helplessness and demoralization has engulfed the state governments, and their power utility organizations. Technological capabilities of the central public sector undertakings and Navaratna companies were badly eroded, as they have drifted away from the goal of technological self—reliance and started playing for the stock markets. CEA, the federal authority that was supposed to guide the country on power development policies has been totally paralyzed.

The search for a global JV partner by PFCCL, which presently enjoys a virtual monopoly hold on power development, is proof for the total policy vacuum that has engulfed India's power sector. The working group for power sector constituted by the Planning Commission for twelfth plan has prepared and submitted its report under the prevailing situation of total policy anarchy: State governments and utility organizations and regulatory bodies under them had virtually no role in their preparation.

---

*   Based on article published in the Passline, January 2013

INDAIN RAILWAYS:
IN SEARCH FOR A NEW VISION*

In December 2009, Mamata Banerji presented in the Indian Parliament the Vision 2020 document for Indian Railways (IR). In the introductory part of this document she had stated: "When I was the Railway Minister last time (1999-2001), Indian Railways was the second largest railway network under a single management in the world in terms of route length, after the Russian Railways. It has now slipped to the third position. Our Vision is to put it on the road to regain the Number Two position in the coming decade and thereafter gain the Number One position in the subsequent decades not just in size, but in every other significant respect."

This, indeed, was a grandiose vision, not only about IR but also about the Minister herself. Within two years, after presenting her vision document, Mamata shifted to Kolkata and since then, she has been ruling over IR from the Writers Building, with the help of her nominee railway minister, Trivedi. Mamata is now unhappy over her nominee's performance: First, he did not do enough for West Bengal and secondly he had proposed a seemingly unpopular revision of rail tariffs, in consultation with her arch rival, Pranab Mukherjee. The good old critics of Mamata from left, right and center, now have their last laugh over her vision document,

ORGANISATIONAL STRUCTURE

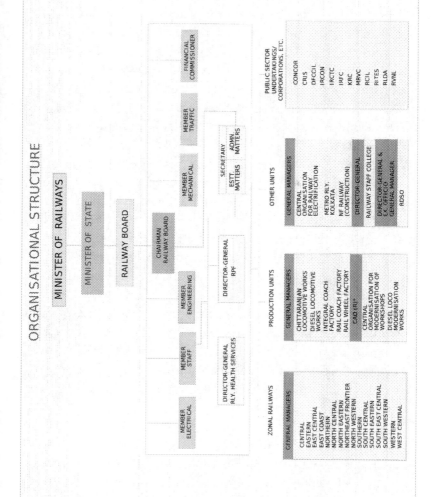

MINISTER OF RAILWAYS

MINISTER OF STATE

RAILWAY BOARD

CHAIRMAN RAILWAY BOARD

| MEMBER ELECTRICAL | MEMBER STAFF | MEMBER ENGINEERING | MEMBER MECHANICAL | MEMBER TRAFFIC | FINANCIAL COMMISSIONER |

DIRECTOR-GENERAL RLY. HEALTH SERVICES

DIRECTOR-GENERAL RPF

SECRETARY

ESTT. MATTERS — ADMN. MATTERS

ZONAL RAILWAYS

GENERAL MANAGERS

CENTRAL
EASTERN
EAST CENTRAL
EAST COAST
NORTHERN
NORTH CENTRAL
NORTH EASTERN
NORTHEAST FRONTIER
NORTH WESTERN
SOUTHERN
SOUTH CENTRAL
SOUTH EASTERN
SOUTH EAST CENTRAL
SOUTH WESTERN
WESTERN
WEST CENTRAL

PRODUCTION UNITS

GENERAL MANAGERS

CHITTARANJAN LOCOMOTIVE WORKS
DIESEL LOCOMOTIVE WORKS
INTEGRAL COACH FACTORY
RAIL COACH FACTORY
RAIL WHEEL FACTORY

CAO (R)*

CENTRAL ORGANISATION FOR MODERNISATION OF WORKSHOPS

DIESEL LOCO MODERNISATION WORKS

OTHER UNITS

GENERAL MANAGERS

CENTRAL ORGANISATION FOR RAILWAY ELECTRIFICATION

METRO RLY, KOLKATA

NF RAILWAY (CONSTRUCTION)

DIRECTOR-GENERAL

RAILWAY STAFF COLLEGE

DIRECTOR-GENERAL & EX. OFFICIO GENERAL MANAGER

RDSO

PUBLIC SECTOR UNDERTAKINGS/ CORPORATIONS, ETC.

CONCOR
CRIS
DFCCIL
IRCON
IRCTC
IRFC
KRC
MRVC
RCIL
RITES
RLDA
RVNL

Indian railway ministers, as a rule, play populist games and try to do something extra for their native states. Mamata was no exemption, despite her tall talk on Vision 2020. Foreign experts and consultants have made dozens of proposals for reforming IR, as part of restructuring the national economy. However, they remained on paper, like the Vision 2020. The only agenda that got implemented, related to staff reduction: As a result, IR suffers from under-staffing today, in terms of quality as well as quantity: Present staff strength is around 14 lakh, two to three lakh less, compared to two decades ago. Last year, 80,000 new hands were recruited anew, and the current budget targets inducting one lakh new employees.

Manpower in IR was growing pretty slow even in the past, compared to its galloping output. True, with higher train speeds and better technologies, labor productivity increases. However, the historical data, presented in the chart "Indices of Growth", show that, there was a 12 fold increase in output, in terms of passenger and goods traffic, with human resources stagnating or increasing only marginally. Not only staff strength but also the route kilometer length of IR has registered only a marginal increase after national independence. In Kerala, we had experienced a big improvement in rail traffic, but that is not the case with most other states. Very few Indian villages and towns in India got connected to the rail after the British left the subcontinent.

Rail penetration in the country continues to be far below the international experience, on the basis of geographical area as well as population. India has 71 route km of railway per million people, and 19 r-km per 1000 sqkm. This is far below that of USA (803/22), France (603/63), Germany (520/117) or Japan (192/63). China was far behind India in rail penetration, but it has more than doubled its route rail length after independence to around 65,000 KM. It may be noted, however, that India was making large investments in doubling of lines as well as in gauge conversion. IR could increase the productivity of its manpower with the help of such improvements in track and related communications systems, as well as higher capacity traction equipment.

Express and long distance trains as well as suburban trains were the major contributors for the 12 fold increase in the output of IR with relatively fewer employees. Quality of service as well as law and order on the tracks and stations were the major causalities in this blind pursuit for higher and higher worker productivity. A railway employee was a respected citizen during British days and even his modest quarters were looked up on with respect by common people. All these have changed now and railway employees were considerably devalued, socially, within the span of a generation.

IR has succeeded in sustaining its relatively good safety records; however crime rates were steadily increasing in recent years. People in general are unhappy with IR, despite its lower costs and more comfortable travel in comparison with alternatives. Dirty coaches, over-crowded and ill-maintained railway stations with extremely poor civic amenities, and not-so-polite employees whose services are strictly rationed, are the order of the day. Indian railway stations were noted for their safety, security, dignified environment, neatness all round and even good quality tasty food.

With large scale retrenchment, stress on long distance express trains and neglect of passenger trains a large number of our railway stations in the rural areas bear a deserted look, today. In the good old days, even the wayside stations were offering parcel booking services to anywhere in India, and had certain minimal go-down facilities. They have mostly disappeared, now. Railway stations in our rural districts are dying a natural death: their assets and facilities could be of use and economic relevance to local populations, if they are salvaged and properly maintained.

Indian Railways were created out of the numerous small rail systems, constructed by British East India Company, and the numerous other companies floated by foreigners. This imaginative PPP adventure of eighteenth century had set up the first rail system in the country in 1853, just four years before Sipoy Mutiny or the First War of Indian Independence. These decentralized initiatives were close to the local communities and local environment in their own ways and for their own reasons. There were numerous mergers and acquisitions of these small ventures, later, and spanning the two centuries: IR and its organization in the present form had evolved over the last six decades of national independence.

IR, as on now, (see Chart) is a complex organization and provides work space for some 14 lakh employees: They work in numerous enterprises, organizations and departments with varied objectives, occupations and assignments that are of great relevance to the national economy. Thanks to its historical background, IR happens to be the father and mother of not only most engineering disciplines in the country, but also of numerous non-engineering professions such as accountancy, project planning, economics, project financing, and even information technology. IR has contributed to the self-reliance of our national economy in a big way, and is a major resource for industrial development.

IR looks like a leviathan and is a bureaucratic organization, presided over by a cabinet minister, supported by one or two ministers of state, and then the Railway Board, its Chairman and half a dozen board members etc etc, and all connected up in series and in parallel. There are fifteen zonal railways, each administered by a General Manger, who looks after the construction and operation of rail lines and related systems of the zone. The nature and number of complaints with regard to their performance indicate that they will perform far better, if re-organized state-wise as in the case of P&T, BSNL, DD, CEA and Electricity Boards etc, and several other Federal Government functions.

It will be even better, if these state-wise organizations are then converted into public sector undertakings with equal shareholding by IR on behalf of Central Government and then by the concerned State Governments, as in the case of Delhi or Chennai Metro. A full fledged rail Minster and a skeletal rail department in every state, for servicing and supporting this joint enterprise will greatly enhance the policy planning capacity at the state level, with regard to rail development as well as planning of the transportation sector. As on now, the state governments have very little expertise in these sectors. This sort of basic reforms will bring the administration of our massive on-rail resources, closer to the people, and the elected Governments at the state as well as lower levels.

Production units of IR under the General Managers, Public Sector Units like CONCOR, CRIS, IRCON, IRCTC, RITES, IRFC, as well as RDSO, as well as the R&D organization of IR should continue their autonomous existence as on now, and they should expand and diversify as necessary. Central Government and the Railway Board will be better placed to prioritize and monitor the work programs of these more important strategic organizations from a national perspective. They could effectively monitor the performance of the railways at the state level, but will be relieved from attending to minor responsibilities related to their day to day operations. IR will enter a phase of centralized policy making and decentralized administration: It has all the systems and procedures as well as checks and balances needed for this transformation, quickly and effectively. No external consultancy, Indian or foreign, will be needed for the purpose.

State governments will be only happy to share the responsibility of rail development in the country. Central Government could play its visionary role far more effectively. Business will be rewarded with a world class rail infrastructure. Workers and trade unions may not raise objections, so long as their rights and perks are protected. What is needed is a change in our mind-set to accept the participation of State Governments in the management of our national rail network. That sort of participation will be far more desirable, practical, and productive than all sorts of PPP models that are being designed and contemplated, now.

---

*   Published in the Passline of March, 2012.

NUCLEAR POWER DEVELOPMENT: A PATRIOTIC PERSPECTIVE*

Nuclear electricity plays an increasing role in grid power development in developed countries, and the trend is likely to continue. Thanks to the complex nature of the technology, that demands close regulation at the national as well as global levels, only large economies with pretty high level of state intervention capabilities could afford its development: Most developing countries are, thus, denied the benefits of this relatively new source of energy.

USA has a big lead in reactor technologies (as is the case of all areas of frontier technologies) and a majority of nuclear reactors, operating in the world today, are of US make or made under US license. It tries to retain reactor technology as its natural monopoly, and uses the unjust regimes of Nuclear Non-proliferation Treaty (NPT) and Nuclear Suppliers Group (NSG) for this purpose.

Indian nuclear program, based on the atoms for peace policy of Nehru days, has made tremendous strides in the peaceful applications of nuclear energy; in health, agriculture, industries and power generation. Eighteen power reactors of total capacity 4460 MW designed, manufactured and fuelled by us are safely working for several years in six power plants, located in six different states of our union republic:

Five more are getting ready for commissioning, including a Thorium based Fast Breeder Reactor of 570 MW.

Our PHWR reactors of 220 MW, 540 MW, and 700 MW ratings are internationally well accepted as safe, robust, efficient and cost effective. We are well advanced in the futuristic breeder technology using Thorium, the exclusive fuel resource of great relevance to our country. DAE has a dozen specialist organizations, dealing with diverse aspects of nuclear technologies with a manpower base of around 50,000. India is a major non-weapon nuclear power, respected for its well integrated technological capabilities, and in this respect, shares a ring-side seat among the comity of nations, along with USA, Russia, France and China.

The three stage nuclear power development program, envisaged by DAE, had targeted for 29460 MW of nuclear power by the year 2022, 62,900 MW by 2032, and 274560 MW by 2052 (targets of 2001). Breeder technology using our own Thorium resources is the unique feature of India's three stage program, which has, by and large, stood the test of time. Even India's Business classes, like Tatas, Birlas or Ambanis could play a role in this national endeavour, if they shed their comprodorial outlook and aspirations.

India never had a serious nuclear weapons program: the two test explosions by the country, one by Indira Gandhi and the other by Vajpayee as Prime Minister, were aberrations to the atom for peace policy formulated by Nehru. However, these were used as alibis for treating India like a nuclear Pariah, by USA, using the unjust NPT-NSG regime under its command. During those cold war years, Soviet Union came forward to help India in setting up the Kudankulam power plant, on extremely favourable terms and conditions, and as an integral part of its own national program.

Implementing this program, along with its vision and targets, may be accepted as a national platform. The organizational structures developed over a period of time, may be reviewed and revised as necessary by the Indian Parliament, and all necessary support by way of material, financial and policy inputs ensured for its systematic implementation. State governments, members of Indian parliament and all patriotic sections of the Indian people should take special interest in this program of great national importance.

The ongoing nuclear power program, the related organizational infrastructure, and human resources base were developed at enormous cost to the national economy, and represent a large investment of great relevance and value for our future. No deal or treaty with foreign countries or change in statutes should affect the efficacy and integrity of this national program or destabilize the structures that were created in the long term benefits of our country.

India, like the USA, is an equal member of UN-IAEA and should take the initiative for opening it up, and strive to liberate it from the clutches of US stranglehold and its handmaiden, the Nuclear Suppliers Group, with the help of other countries. Normal international trade in nuclear materials needs to be encouraged, under the supervision of IAEA, which should promote international cooperation in the peaceful applications of atomic energy.

India should use its bi-lateral relationships and diplomatic influence with other countries and group of countries, for a role in the management of IAEA that is commensurate with its expertise and image as the largest non-weapon nuclear country in the developing world.

India should keep its commitments to the exclusive use of nuclear technologies for peaceful purposes and campaign for total nuclear disarmament along with all peace-loving peoples of the world.

---

*   Presented in the seminar at Institution of Engineers Cochin Centre on 24-06-2013

GLOBALISATION AND DOWNSIZING OF GOVERNMENT*

State is an object of resentment, irrespective of ideologies. Anarchists see it as the origin of crimes, businessmen blame it for economic sins, socialists see it as an instrument of coercion, and religions had always resisted its influence over human psyche. Market economists as well as Marxists had wished its withering away, for long. But the institution continues to grow and expand its role in human development.

World Development Report 1997 of the World Bank had its focus on 'the State in Changing World' and noted: Over the last century the size and scope of government have expanded enormously, particularly in the industrial countries. According to its estimates, total government expenditure in OECD countries was less than ten percent of their GDP in 1870. This had steadily grown five fold, to nearly fifty percent by 1995. Critics of market economics had pointed out even earlier that, State had continued to grow in these countries even during eighties and nineties, despite the tall talks of Thatherism and Reagnomics and had held this in support of their theories on State Monopoly Capitalism and Industrial-Military complexes. Expansion and enrichment of the role of State on either side of the cold war however, was characterised as proof of convergence of socio-political systems, by Professor Galbrieth and others of the liberal tradition.

In developing countries that took to mixed economies, State was seen as a critical resource for socio-economic development, as a matter of political consensus. According to WDR-1997, central government expenditure in developing countries was just fifteen percent of their GDP in 1960 which had nearly doubled up by 1990. In the Indian economy, total government expenditure had peaked to 26 percent of GDP by 1991 and then started declining, thanks to economic reforms. It was argued that, due to economic planning and growth of public sector organisations, India was over-administered and down-sizing of Government at every level was the first step toward faster development.

Fallacy of this argument will be even clearer, when we consider the numerical size of Governments in industrial countries. USA with a population base of 265 million had 24 million Government employees in 2002, including its armed forces, or some 91employeess per 1000 population. India with 1100 Million people had only 13 million Government employees or about twelve per thousand people. India is a very thinly administered country and combined with the lower efficiencies at every level, Indian State is no match to that of USA. Even a casual look at the two societies will reinforce this statistical evidence. But, public opinion in India had accepted uncritically the prescriptions for the downsizing of Indian State, when industrial countries, including USA, continue to move in opposite direction.

Further, more than 16 percent of the working people in USA were directly employed by Government in 2002;

the corresponding figure for India was less than 4 percent. Relative sizes of public employment and distribution of employees at various levels of governance in the two countries make interesting comparisons. Data compiled by US Labour Bureau and Economic Review of Indian Government are analysed in table below:

PUBLIC EMPLOYMENT AT DIFFERENT LEVELS OF GOVERNMENT: YEAR 2002		
	USA	INDIA
Employees per 1000 Population		
Federal/Central	20	3
State Governments	19	7
Local Governments	52	2
TOTAL	91	12
Percent Distribution		
Federal/Central	22	25
State Governments	21	58
Local Governments	57	17
TOTAL	100	100

The table throws some light on the structural efficacy of Indian State, compared to its US Counterpart: Governance at all levels is week in India, compared to that in USA. In terms employees per 1000 population, US Federal Government was nearly seven times stronger. State Governments in USA had nearly three times more employees compared to Indian States on a population basis. State and Federal Governments were thus of nearly same size in USA whereas, State Governments in India had more than double the strength of Central Government.

Local Self Governments, with less than two employees per thousand people, are the weakest links of State power in India. They are mere pigmies compared to their US compartments, which constitute a formidable part of US State power. With 52 employees per 1000 population, local governments in USA, are the providers of a variety of community services at the street level: education, health, social security, human resources development, local transport, trade, tourism atdl.

Despite Gandhian dreams of Gram-Swaraj, JP movement of seventies, constitutional amendments of 1991 and repeated demands and promises by the Left and the Right, Local Governments were a virtual non-starter in our Union Republic. And now, we are downsizing Government as a whole. Is it the right response to the second wave of globalisation, triggered in by countries, far more powerful than ours?

---

*   Published in the Passline of January 2004

CONTAINING CORRUPTION: A HISTORICAL PERSPECTIVE*

Our society continues to be semi-feudal even
after six decades of independent development.
Indian state is far more authoritarian and corrupt
compared to its counterparts in developed
countries. That is typical of developing societies,
and the situation can be changed only by
strengthening the state through an extensive
process of democratic decentralization. However,
the intelligentsia and other sections of our elite
classes look at democratic decentralization of
governance and participative management
of corporates as a threat to their hegemonic
stranglehold over society. They spread the illusion
that, democracy is the root cause of corruption
and inefficiency and the situation could be
saved only by extensive policing by Lokpal like
institutions, which will be naturally dominated
and controlled by them. This article looks at
Anna Hazare movement based on the historical
experience of nations and nation states.

Entire nation seems to be obsessed with the issue of
corruption and debating on having omnipotent institutions
of Lokpal at the Central and State levels for policing over the
corrupt state machinery. An NGO under the banner, India

Against Corruption (IAC) (www.indiaagainstcorruption. org) and its leaders, a group of eminent citizens describing themselves as India's civic society, are the promoters of Anna Hazare. They are supported by our English speaking media, visual as well as print, generally patronized by the elite classes living in Indian metros. National debates and discussions triggered by them had focused entirely on the policing of corruption, with the help of a large establishment, to be created anew. Little is being discussed about how to prevent or at least minimize the incidence of corruption: If policing were a solution, India could have been a corruption-free nation, long long ago.

The IAC was jointly promoted by the Fifth Estate Movement (www.5thpillar.org), another recently promoted NGO, mostly powered by NRI funds, and the Indian Chapter of Transparency International (TI), an NGO established in 1993 and head-quartered in Berlin: The TI (www.transparency.org) seems to be part the global political initiative of European Union (EU) and claim themselves to be a Global Coalition Against Corruption. Its Indian Chapter, Transparency International India (TII) " is part of the Asia Pacific forum comprising 20 nations that include China, Sri Lanka, Bangladesh, Pakistan, Maldives and others." The TII (www.transparencyindia. org), according to its website "is a non-government, non-party and not-for-profit organization of Indian citizens with professional, social, industrial or academic experience seeking to promote transparent and ethical governance and to eradicate corruption".

TII seems to be intensely patronized by Navaratna CPSUs and has zonal offices in almost all Northern states. The Lokpal movement, spearheaded by an NGO network jointly promoted by TII and the more recent Fifth Estate Movement in Southern states has several similarities with the recent reform movements staged in the Arab world, in style as well as content. It has opened up a Pandora's box, and the massive media build-up managed by it within a few weeks, has greatly embarrassed and shaken up the Indian Establishment: The ruling coalition as well as the opposition political coalitions are under compulsion to take a stand on the galloping corruption in the country, as a result of the two decades old economic reforms and trade liberalization program.

Prime Minister Dr. Manmohan Singh has come out in defense of his Government, saying that his Government was being (wrongly) described as the most corrupt in India's history. He has blamed the media as well as the institutions like CAG for playing the accuser, the prosecutor and the judge at the same time. He has told the press that, there was no question of short-circuiting the Parliamentary process of legislation and bringing the PMO under the scanner of the new Lokpal as demanded by the NGOs. He was quite right in upholding the values of parliamentary democracy and in not yielding to the demands by the international network of NGOs, well-orchestrated by a section of the local and foreign media. He had asserted that Lokpal was not a panacea and that there was no question of going back to the era of license-permit raj or ushering in a new era of police raj, for eliminating corruption. In his view, the unique identification project of UIDAI would "discover a new pathway to eliminate corruption and leakages in the management and distribution of various subsidies to which the people are entitled."

By such assertions, Prime Minister was trying to win back the confidence of India's elite classes on one hand and the global financial institutions on the other: But they are largely illogical and hardly supported by facts. For example, there was little logic in characterizing the Nehru era of planned development as mere license-permit raj: It had helped to build the technological as well as political foundations of modern India, despite its several deficiencies. Instead of reforming it to the real needs of the country, similar to what China had done, Dr. Singh & Co implemented reform packages recommended by IBRD experts that had opened up the flood gates of corruption in almost all sectors of national economy. His reference to police Raj was an obvious diatribe on the Chinese or Socialist model development which is getting better and better acceptance today, in the context the current global crisis. Dr. Singh seems to argue that parliamentary democracy, as presently practiced in India is a great virtue and that corruption is very much a part of the deal. However, this is a grossly misleading formulation and an irresponsible one for the Prime Minister.

All developed countries practice parliamentary democracy in one form or the other, and their governments are counted to be more transparent and free from corruption in their dealings with the general public as well as business. True, perceptions on corruption and transparency as well as their indexation by TI and their affiliates are likely to be influenced by their free-market culture. Despite possible distortions, indexes arrived at in their studies and reports may be counted as reflections of reality. TI Report of 2010 evaluated the transparency or Corruption (Free) Perception Index of 178 countries on a 10 to 1 scale, using the reports of World Bank and other international institutions as inputs. In this report, Denmark, New Zealand and Singapore tops the list with an equal score of 9.3, where as Somalia (1.1), Myanmar (1.4) and Afghanistan (1.4) are at the bottom of the scale. Transparency indexes for selected countries, based on this report, are reproduced in the table for enabling a critical review.

Transparency Index of Selected Countries for 2010 as Estimated by TI		
Country	Composite Score by TI	Rank
Denmark	9.3	1
Norway	8.6	10
Hongkong	8.4	13
Germany	7.9	15
UK	7.6	20
USA	7.1	22
Taiwan	5.8	33
South Korea	5.4	39
Italy	3.9	67
Cuba	3.7	69
China	3.5	78
India	3.3	87
Egypt	3.1	98
Bangladesh	2.4	134
Pakistan	2.3	143
Russia	2.1	154
Source TI Report 2011		

Indian States: Corruption Index in 2005 estimated by TI		
State	Index	Rank
Kerala	240	1
Himachal	301	2
Gujarat	417	3
Andhra Pradesh	421	4
Maharshtra	433	5
Chattisgarh	445	6
Punjab	459	7
West Bengal	461	8
Orissa	475	9
Uttar Pradesh	491	10
Delhi	496	11
Tamilnadu	509	12
Haryana	516	13
Jharkand	520	14
Assam	542	15
Rajasthan	543	16
Karnataka	576	17
Madhya Pradesh	584	18
Jammu and Kashmir	655	19
Bihar	696	20
Source: India Corruption Study 2005 by TI		

Despite its claims as World's largest democracy, India with a transparency rank of 87 and score of 3.1, is far more corrupt, compared to the developed countries with market economies and practicing parliamentary democracy. Hong-Kong and Taiwan are placed several notches above India. None of these countries has Lokpal-type institutions for the policing of corruption, as pleaded for by India's Civic Society people. However, unlike India, USA has a genuine federal constitution that functions, and the governments of member states, together with an efficient network of local self-governments are accountable to people at large, for most part of their social and economic needs. US Senate and Congress, unlike Indian Loksabha and Rajyasabha, debate and discuss not only bare laws, but also policies and programs, rather threadbare. In India, the recent massive economic reforms and restructuring programs were implemented with very little or no consultations with the Parliament and member states of the Union Republic.

Governing systems in European countries are basically not much different from that of USA. They have, in addition, a system of industrial democracy that ensures the participation of workers in corporate management. Possibly, that is why EU countries, in general, have a better transparency score than USA. It may be noted from the table that, apart from Hong Kong and Cuba, even mainland China were assessed by TI, as more transparent and less corrupt compared to India. All these facts simply exposes the hollowness of Dr. Singh's argument that, democracy and corruption go together and that nothing much could be done other than waiting for deliverance by the UIDAI, an authoritarian project and institution, conceived by our elite classes with the support and blessings of IBRD and other related institutions.

Despite the federal character of our constitution, our Government in Delhi has transformed itself into an all powerful Central Government, that is turning less and less transparent in policy making and project implementation, under the influence of monopoly capital and global finance. Recommendations for recasting the present Center-State relations on more rational and democratic lines, by several commissions and reform panels, including the latest one dedicated for the purpose, were simply shelved by Dr. Singh & Co under advice from the elite classes that support him. Worker participation in corporate management is a directive principle of Indian constitution from the days of Indira Gandhi. But successive governments have ignored its implementation with the exemption of the short-lived VP Singh Government. A bill drafted for this purpose is pending in the Rajyasabha for more than two decades waiting for its final disposal. Democratic decentralization of governance as well as participative management of corporate institutions will dramatically improve the transparency as well as the efficacy of the Indian State and also bring down the incidence of corruption in a big way. That is what should learn from the historical experience of developed countries.

The vast scope for minimizing or eliminating corruption with the help of democratic reforms is indicated by the comparative corruption indexes, compiled for various states by the Transparency International India (TII). Results of this corruption study done with British assistance, some six years ago, are summarized in a second table. Bihar with an index of 696 was found to be the most corrupt state in 2005 and Kerala the least corrupt with an index of 240. Kerala is far advanced compared to other states, not only in the empowerment of local governments, but also in literacy, penetration of media, incidence of class and mass organizations, and awareness democratic rights among the people. There are plenty of lessons to be learned or simply copied from each other by the Indian states, in order to prevent or minimize corruption at various levels of governance.

Unfortunately, the eminent citizens, non-resident Indians and those of the elite classes that have come together and launched the India Against Corruption Movement of Anna Hazare are not bothered about the possibilities of democratic reforms, that could contain and minimize corruption at various levels, but also strengthen the developmental role of the Indian state. The proposed omnipresent and omnipotent Lokpal institutions proposed by by them are closer to the fascist dreams of disciplining the societies under their hegemony. It has nothing to do with the democratic aspirations of our people and may turnout to be a mirage of little social significance.

---

*   Published in the Passline of September, 2011

THIRD FRONT
AND RE-ENVISIONING OF
INDIAN UNITY *

The notion of a third front of regional parties led by the left and challenging the two fronts led by the so called national parties, had an inspiring and colorful take off during the fifteenth Loksabha elections. However, the very idea was looked down as plague by our elite classes. The main stream media had refused even to debate on the possibilities of and prospects of such an alternative. And under the heat of real politics it simply vanished like a rainbow: The protagonists of the idea were criticized and ridiculed for lack of vision and political experience. Revolutionary ideas are nothing but beautiful dreams, and we keep striving for their realization. The Indian State is degenerating rather rapidly and the search for an alternative system of governance for the Union Republic could hardly be postponed.

Indian National Congress had long outlived its role as the leader of national liberation: the bogus Gandhi mantle on the person of its President has lost most of its magical powers. BJP holds out Ram as a political trump card, but its efficacy has been greatly eroded by far lesser gods of more recent origin. Both Congress and BJP have lost most of their mass appeal, and regional parties that are close to the people at large are seen deserting these so called national parties, one after the other.

Our elite classes generally look down on regional parties: They are considered to be of little or no national importance. Regional parties even use all India labels, in order to enhance their repute, respectability and public acceptance. Nevertheless, relevance of regional parties has steadily increased, thanks to the failures of the national parties to live up to the expectations of common people. And today, they play a substantially large role in governing our Union Republic. Majority of Indian States are ruled, today, not by the national parties, but by regional parties or political coalitions led by them. Congress and BJP, the two national parties patronized by the elite classes in order to develop a stable two party system of governance, wield political power only in fewer number of member states of the Union Republic.

Under our federal constitution, state governments are accountable for most part of development administration and governance, including the delivery of public goods like policing and street level security. Division of responsibilities among Central, State and Local Self Government Institutions is somewhat water-tight in our country, and not seamless as it should be, and as practiced in developed democracies elsewhere. As a consequence, there are numerous blind spots in our system of governance: The totally confused response to the 26/11 terror strike on Mumbai should serve as an eye opener in this regard.

Obviously, there is a gross mismatch between the responsibilities assigned to state Governments and the material resources at their disposal for discharging them. This mismatch has widened over the past years. State governments elected by the people and accountable to them, are hardly equipped to live up to their expectations regarding material and cultural development. Public institutions under them are totally ill-equipped and grossly underdeveloped compared to their counterparts at the Centre. Thanks to near total financial dependency, state governments find it impossible to launch meaningful capacity building programs and HRD projects of their own. This had precipitated a sort of self-aggravating dichotomy in Indian polity, which has now assumed alarming proportions, especially in the context of the recent economic reforms and structural adjustments.

Centralized policy making and decentralized administration are, no doubt, the golden principles of modern management; in business as well as in government. However, such a division of responsibilities in our federal constitution has not helped in developing a healthy Centre-State relationship. Due to the near-total financial dependency and lack of grass-root level democracy, decentralized administration at the state and lower levels has remained a mere pipe dream. Centralized policy making, on the other hand had served in the past to a large extent, the twin objectives of protecting the national economy from neo-colonial exploitation, as well as optimum use of internal resources.

After national independence, the Government in Delhi had substantially expanded its developmental role, by opening up new technical departments, several Central Public Sector Enterprises (CPSEs) or the so called *Navaratna* companies, as well as a vast network of S&T organizations: Indian Parliament, Planning Commission, the National Development Council (NDC) etc were serving as watch dogs over this large institutional network in broader national interests. Statesmen like the great Rajaji had condemned this elaborate policy making apparatus as license-permit-quota raj: Nevertheless, it had helped the country in making rapid technological strides in several sectors and in pursuing an independent foreign policy. However, capacity building of this magnitude did not take place at the state level due to a variety of reasons, including historical ones like bureaucratic hangover from the colonial administration in Delhi, as well as vested interests of big business houses.

These institutional arrangements intended for formulation of policies based on national consensus have been either destroyed or have undergone fundamental changes in recent times, thanks to the structural adjustment programs. Footloose bureaucrats and corrupt politicians decide on national policies and programs today, with little or no formal consultations at the national level and with state governments. The notorious nuclear deal with US was initiated by the Indian Ambassador in USA, and not by the atomic energy establishment, energy and power departments, or the Central Electricity Authority. There were no consultations, whatsoever, with the state governments either: They are accountable for the street level supply of grid electricity and no nuclear power plant could be built on Indian soil without their permission and cooperation!

Electricity Act 2003, replacing the old act of 1948, was rushed through, despite serious objections raised by several state governments. Our country has no worthwhile power policy today, and the main concern of the union power ministry is the assigning of EPC contracts for super power stations in locations, finalized by it through all sorts dubious mechanisms. All these have virtually destabilized grid power development in the country, leading to widespread shortages and steep increases in electricity prices. Ministry for telecoms has given up the time-tested national policy of capacity expansion based on an integrated program of technology development and local manufacture. Its only responsibility today is to auction off market rights for telecom operations and for this purpose we do not really require a union ministry in Delhi.

Signing of WTO agreement, the arbitrary withdrawal of agricultural subsidies by Central Government and opening up of free trade agreements have destabilized Indian farms, opening up an era of massive farmer suicides. Several such examples of arbitrary policy changes by central government could be cited, including those related to defense policies and defense contracts, where the central government had abdicated or misused the policy making authority vested with it, in national interests.

Thanks to such numerous acts of omissions and commissions on the policy front, the very institution of central government has lost its moral authority over state governments, and along with it most of its patriotic credentials, earned and accumulated during the era of national planning and consensus, initiated under the leadership of Jawaharlal Nehru. This should be a matter of great political concern for a multinational country of continental proportions.

The massive distortions that have crept into Centre-State relations, the working of our federal constitution and Indian polity at large, need urgent correction in the best interests of our people. Initiatives for this will not come from the so called national parties, Congress or BJP. Only a united front of the regional parties, who are in real charge of governance or aspiring for it, and covering a sizable part of Indian population, could be expected to take on such initiatives. The ten parties that have sponsored the third front in the present Loksabha elections have underlined the need for a serious review of the working of the Indian constitutions in general and Central-State relations in particular: Some of them have even published detailed discussions papers on the subject on the very eve of the elections.

These more serious aspects of Indian democracy and Indian polity are hardly discussed by our mainstream media. Pessimistic forecasts about the emerging third front of regional parties are the order of the day. Regional parties are often described as a motley crowd with no vision or objectives and without a Prime Minister candidate. They underplay the fact that, the Prime Minister candidate of Congress is not even contesting the elections. And, as alleged by the present leader of opposition in Parliament, Manmohan was the weakest among Indian Prime Ministers: It is common knowledge, that he was back-seat driven by an extensive PMO headed by a minister and controlled by numerous commissions and committees that were either unconstitutional or extra-constitutional. Five year term of UPA and Manmohan has proved beyond reasonable doubt that, our Union Republic barely needs a popular Prime Minister for its survival!

Even in the absence of a Charismatic Prime Minister, the third front Government could hold the country together in a far more satisfactory manner, by making use of constitutional entities like the Inter State Council. It could be effectively used in the formulation of national policies and for evolving consensus decisions on controversial issues; and its decisions need to be made binding on the Central Government. Even subject wise Inter State Councils could be established, if found necessary, as recommended in 2002 by Justice Venkitachelliah in his capacity as the Chairman of the National Committee for Reviewing the Working of the Constitution. Planning Commission could strengthen its federal character by working as the executive body of the National Development Council, and making this august body accountable to the Inter State Council.

Central Government organizations could develop a federal character by establishing state level subsidiaries and affiliates, as part of a much needed capacity building program at the regional level. Major states could be invited, in turn, to participate in the corporate management of Navaratna companies, at the board level. A third front of the regional parties, which are already participating in the governance of the country in a big way, are well equipped to formulate such alternative policies and programs and bring the Central Government administration closer to the people, help it shed its imperial pretensions, and liberate it from the stranglehold of global monopolists.

Unity in diversity as reflected in *janaganamana* is the hallmark of Indian polity. Coming together of the regional parties around an alternative development perspective could be a turning point in Indian history. And, the third front that is just emerging, is sure to re-envision Indian unity in an altogether different perspective; a perspective that is far more realistic and relatively free from financial and religious fundamentalism.

---

* Prepared in April 2009 as campaign document for the fifteenth Loksabha elections

VISION KERALA 2025: ANOTHER EXERCISE IN FUTILITY*

Confederation of Indian Industries (CII), founded over 112 years ago, is India's premier business association. Its Kerala State Council has brought out a vision document for the State. The document was prepared with the help of a professional consultancy organisation and was released by VS Achuthananandan, the Chief Minister of Kerala, in a ceremonial function held last month at Kochi. The 57 page full report of the consultant could be seen at *www.visionkerala2025.in*

CII claims to represent Indian business: It has 63 offices in India, eight overseas offices and institutional partnerships with 271 counterpart organisations in 100 countries. It has a direct membership of over 7000 organisations from the private as well as public sectors, including SMEs and MNCs and an indirect membership of over 90,000 companies and around 360 national, regional and sectoral associations. Unlike the Federation of Indian Chambers of Commerce and Industries (FICCI), representing large business houses, CII has a broad based and diffused membership. Possibly that is why Vision Kerala 2025 sounds more like a political platform with all sort of slogans and jargons for attracting public attention.

The document envisions: By 2025, Kerala would be a vibrant, sustainable modern State providing its citizens globally comparable quality of life and opportunities to excel in their chosen walk of life. The consultants, M/s ICRA Management Consulting Services (IMaCS), who prepared this vision document, has also proposed an action plan in three parts for realizing this vision: During the first stage, lasting six to seven months the State Government *should partner with CII to catalyse public opinion and evolve over a consensus on the key vision themes for facilitating the transfer of ownership of the vision to all key stake holders and develop an implementation plan focussing on specific initiatives.* That is a tall order for a State Government that has come to power through an electoral process as per the Indian constitution and accountable to the State legislature! Such tall postures by the CII and its mandated Consultant, to say the least, are laughable! However, we will examine here, briefly, some of the vision themes, the so called stake holders and initiatives assigned to them in the vision document.

Vision Kerala 2025 introduces the so called key vision themes under, (1) Green and sustainable development, (2) opportunities for all, (3) globally comparable quality of life, (4) Global engagement, and (5) transparency in government and administration. Themes and sub-themes are discussed, as if Kerala is a sovereign State constituting a sovereign economy. The document makes frequent references to global economy and global development, but their is little mention about the Union Republic, the existence of a national market, linkages with the national economy, the impact of national policies and the reality of an all pervasive Central-State relations. Discussions and analysis that do not take into account these realities cannot claim even academic relevance, leave alone practical importance.

Let us take the visions around agriculture. Crisis in agriculture is an all India phenomenon and farmers in Kerala respond to this crisis by switching to more money yielding crops. When the yield of cash incomes, per unit area of farm land or per person engaged in farming in Kerala, is nearly three times the all India average, there is no point in talking about the agrarian crisis in Kerala in isolation. Productivity of Kerala farms is generally high compared to all India averages, even for labour intensive crops, but is far below that of countries like China or South Korea. The report is right in recommending modernisation of agriculture through the collective efforts of farmers, in order to overcome the problems of fragmentation of land holdings. However, it is silent on the failure of the existing agriculture cooperatives in the state, numbering over one thousand and with a membership exceeding fifteen million, in realising their declared objective of farm modernisation.

Instant remedies with little bearing on the ground realities, as seen in the case of agriculture, are handed out for the industries sector as well: When there is ample scope for the modernisation, expansion and diversification of already existing heavy electrical engineering industries (TELK, KEL), ship and boat building (Cochin Shipyard and others) or machine tool and other engineering industries (HMT, IL), preference insisted on light engineering industries for the State makes very little sense. The so called green technology and sustainable development are mere abstract political ideas or ideology that makes little practical sense. Any economy tries to develop and build on the strength of what it already has: Business associations are the right agencies to advise governments on such policies and programs: CII should have exercised this privilege, instead of pouring out such bland recommendations based on ideologies of Fourth World theoreticians. In any case, such policies cannot be pursued in a single state of the Union Republic, in isolation. Recommendations on the use of clean fuels like CNG or LNG fall into the very same category: They presuppose the existence of an independent fuel policy for the State of Kerala

Business management methods and tools have their obvious limitations, while handling larger social problems. Other than military dictatorship, there is no way to bypass the political process. The fallacy of looking at Kerala as a sovereign republic was pointed out already. The second fallacy in CII Vision is its concept about the so called Stake Holders: Under a democratic dispensation, the people of the State, individually and collectively are the stake holders. However, the vision document tries to identify the change agents in Kerala society in terms of Stake Holders other than the people of Kerala, as if Kerala Society is an enterprise operating in a global environment or global market. It has identified four stakeholders as the agents for realising the visions, already defined: State Government, industry or business, groups and organised bodies and individuals. And, in the last chapter, the document asks the Government to join hands with the CII for organising discussions on the vision document and get it vetted by the entire people, within six to seven months.

We may forgive the intellectual arrogance of the consultants, who have drawn up this vision document: However, the State Council of CII and its office bearers should have moderated and refrained from rushing to the Government and the Chief Minister with such half-baked ideas and visions of no practical use. This has only adversely affected the credibility of CII as a responsible business association.

Such all embracing prescriptions could have been better submitted to the State Planning Board, while preparing the approach document for five year plans. Some two years ago the State Planning Board was finalising the eleventh plan: Did the Kerala State Council of the CII submit any proposals for consideration by the Planning Board and the Government of Kerala?

Perhaps, an even more relevant question is: Did the State Planning Board consult the CII and other business associations, while formulating the eleventh plan proposals? Industry and business are the salt of the earth and those who manage them should have a legitimate say in the formulation of economic and social policies. It is sad that, such consultations are not the part of our political culture and system of Governance. Politicians and bureaucrats, in our state, are not generally inclined to grant this role to industry associations. And, that is common knowledge. However, those who lead industry associations are more to be blamed for this unhealthy situation.

Business associations are looked upon by their mentors as instruments for public relations and not as tools for partnering development. That is why **Vision Kerala 2025** has ended up as an exercise in futility. It once again proves the urgent need for a paradigm shift: a paradigm shift in the relationship between business associations and state government.

---

*   Published in the Passline, May 2008.

INDUSTRIAL DEVELOPMENT
NEED FOR A PARADIGM SHIFT*

Twelve years ago, in 1996, late EK Nayanar laid the foundation stone for the Industrial Growth Centre (IGC—much larger than Industrial Estates and the predecessor of SEZ—Special Economic Zones) at Kinalur in Koothuparambu Assembly constituency: That was just a month after he took over as LDF Chief Minister of Kerala for a third time. He was to seek election to Kerala assembly, later that year, from that constituency. For the Industries Minster, late Suseela Gopalan, it was a moment of pride to preside over the foundation laying ceremony. As a Member of Parliament, she had put up a stiff fight for two Growth Centre Projects in Kerala: Kannur district was granted the first one and Alapuzha district the second.

I had just taken over as the Non-Executive Chairman of Kerala State Industrial Development Corporation (KSIDC) and Honorary Advisor to the Minister for Industries, and was hardly enthused by the prospects of participating in this inaugural function. But, Amithabh, my young Managing Director was much more enthusiastic than even the Minister: He had contracted for KSIDC the responsibility of implementing IGC Projects, from the previous ministry, a decision which was later reversed, under my insistence. A few hundred acres of land was already acquired with record speed and land cleared of coconut trees for holding the foundation laying ceremony in the prospective constituency of Chief Minister. There were Red rallies all over, daring the trunks of hundreds of coconut trees that were felled on an emergency basis. As the last but one speaker on the occasion, I felt nervous while addressing the milling crowd: IGC being a sort of blind expedition, I was scared of the prospects of facing the very same militant crowd, a few years later.

Twelve years have passed and ministries and ministers have changed twice. But not a single industry worth its salt, has found roots in this tough hostile terrain, despite dozens of kilometres of well laid out roads, thousands of square meters of built up floor area, power, water and related infrastructure. When the present Industries Minister took over, his advisors brought in a Malaysian team who put out the grandiose story of converting Kinalur IGC into a Satellite Township. Nothing is heard of this now, and Kinalur continues to be a hopeless case of IGC like several others. Nevertheless, its fate was a shade better than that of the second IGC that took off later at Chertala: land was acquired, but no other infrastructure has come up except the massive boundary walls. The only industry that has so far come up was the captive sand mining project for the nearby Excel Glass: Local people are now agitating against the breach of promises on industrial development.

IGCs, with their focus on medium scale enterprises, were part of the industrial development program of Central Government, conceived during the early years of economic reforms: They were, in fact, the successors to the industrial estates, mini industrial estates, functional industrial estates, industrial parks etc etc of the pre-reform era for promoting small and medium scale industries. The shift in policy towards foreign companies and large business houses gave birth to, the much larger Special Economic Zones, to be directly administered by Central Government, with State Governments playing only a marginal role. The very concept of SEZ is facing problems now, and a consensus view is evading the country, not only in Parliament but also among the member satcs of the Union Republic. All these post-reform policy innovations were triggered from the simple belief that, plenty of capital was floating around the world, which could be attracted by investor friendly State Governments by identifying and pointing out investment possibilities in their respective regions.

The Global Investment Meet (GIM) of 2003 organised by KSIDC and on behalf of the Industries Minister was one of the most lively business promotion shows, sponsored by any State Government. This two-day event in Kochi, organised at the Meridian and Casino hotels, was inaugurated by Prime Minister Vajpeyee, with Chief Minister AK Antony as the presiding diety and Leader of Opposition VS Achuthanandan delivering an outstanding felicitation speech. Industries department had presented 129 project profiles with a total investment of around Rs.34,000 Crore and covering some 16 industrial sectors (see the summary table extracted from GIM Directory).

Potential investors from all over the country and abroad who turned up in large numbers were well taken care of, entertained and seen off content and satisfied. However, there were hardly any takers for the over-glorified project packages offered by the organisers. GIM organisers saved their face by pointing out the investment announcements made by the Prime Minister, on behalf of the Central Public Sector Units, totalling some 10,000 Crore!

GIM and most of the project profiles brought out by it were the products of wild imagination of our bureaucrats and their foreign consultants. The larger ones were pepped up to catch the imagination of foreign investors and had very little to do with the real needs of people and the possibilities around. For example, the access controlled high-speed corridor or express highway from Thiruvananthapuram to Kasargod (Rs.7000 Crore), had nothing to do with the mass transportation needs of a 550 Km long metro-like region of some 20 million people that was emerging on the Kerala coast. Such concepts imported from Malaysia or Saudi Arabia with extremely low population densities were hardly suited for the Kerala environment. The Petrochemical Complex proposed for North Malabar (Rs.7500 Crore), ready with a feasibility study and letter of intent from the Government of India right from 1999 had died a natural death for lack of follow up. Palazhy Tyres, a disgraced cooperative venture under the leadership of KM Mani, hanging fire for more than a decade, was another project proposal. Power sector proposals included in the GIM package were mere idle dreams of the environmentalist lobby. GIM was shabbily packaged show, lacked seriousness in style and content: It was pretentious and dishonest to the core and as a consequence had eroded the very credibility of Kerala as an investment destination.

The establishment in charge of industrial development in the state, including the industries department in the Secretariat, has degenerated into precious nothing, long long ago. Barring a couple IAS Officers, the permanent bureaucracy in Government has very little expertise in matters related to industrial development. Department of Industries & Commerce, outside the Government secretariat, has lost most of its functional relevance and sense of purpose, despite being the custodian of District Industries Centres (DIC) and Taluk Industrial Centres. DICs have lost their relevance long back and hardly know why they exist: They are not even considered as reliable source of industrial statistics. Kerala State Small Industries Development Corporation Ltd. (Kerala—SIDCO), a pivotal organisation in the old policy framework, exists today mainly for its employees.

IT and Coir are mercifully outside the purview of the department: Kerala Financial Corporation (KFC) that finances the bulk of small scale industries continues to be governed by the Finance Department and industrial development is hardly its concern, even in the good old days. Kerala State Industrial Development Corporation (KSIDC), considered to be the major development arm of State Government, has the Principal Secretary to the Prime Minister as its Super Chairman for more than a decade now, and in the absence of a full time CEO it is hardly accountable to anybody. Then, there is the KINFRA, the numerous other industrial parks specialising in their own way and the new promotional agency, constituted about an year ago, still waiting on its wings to a decent take off. These along with the fifty and odd public sector industries, RIAB, KBIP and other pocket organisations, which are virtually under the control of senior bureaucrats, are managed by the Minister and his personnel staff, who consider themselves as providers and benefactors: They hardly feel the need for dialogue and consultations with the so called captains of industries, industry associations, trade unions or professional bodies.

The large establishment and public sector enterprises under the industry ministry need to be restructured to improve communication within and with the outside world. District Industries Centres and Taluk Industries Centres could be jointly managed along with the local industry associations, and local governments could have a say in this: The Business Centre model as in UK could provide the establishment with extensive interactive linkages with the industry. Industrial Estates could be brought under the joint management of local government and cooperatives of the concerned industrial units.

Cooperatives of the units in Industrial Estates and Parks may be encouraged to take on bigger and broader responsibilities. SIDCO and its warehouses could play a new role under the changed policy frame work: It could initiate projects for setting up super markets, specialising in the supply of engineering materials, mechanical, electrical and electronic components and basic chemicals needed as inputs for a variety of industries. Dependance on the metro cities and Coimbatore or Bangalore for such key inputs is a major reason for the technological backwardness of our manufacturing industry. Sector-wise consolidation of public sector industries and group management could initiate not only joint action among them but also for promote industrial units in private sector.

State Government should end the policy of keeping a distance from the management of Central Public Sector Units: FACT, HMT, CSL, KRL, IRE, HOCL, HNL and others need to be seen as key development resources for the State. Active participation in their BoD and the formulation of their expansion-diversification program could make immense sense.

Development efforts based on IGCs, SEZ and road shows are bound to be a failure. That is the lesson to be learnt from our post-reform experience and we need a paradigm shift. It is not the intention here to lay down any detailed policy frame work. But the paradigm shift should help the establishment in building up its capacity for interacting with the existing industrial infrastructure. And it means: Build on from what we already have, rather than trying to build castles in the air. It does not mean the end of all dreams: Let us first build on our capacity to dream more and more rational dreams.

---

*   Article published in the Passline of April. 2008

RAPID LOSS OF CAPACITY TO GOVERN*

The two monorail projects proposed for Thiruvananthapuram and Kozhikodu will be under the State Public Works Department (State PWD), unlike Kochi Metro, looked after by transport department. A new SPV, with an estimated investment of over Rs. 6000 Crore will be floated for this purpose, under the overall control of the PWD Minister.

Discussions on the choice of administrative department for urban transport development make very little sense in Kerala: Neither PWD nor Transport Department has the professional capacity or competence for even engaging external consultants, global or domestic, to take up feasibility studies or prepare detailed project reports for such infrastructure projects. Both are governed by senior IAS officers, designated as principal secretaries and as innocent about the subject as their political bosses.

True, Kerala PWD has a separate roads and bridges division but it has no expertise on transportation engineering or urban transport development. It has a roads and bridges corporation directly controlled by the minister and presided over by a senior IAS or IPS officer. Unlike the Kerala Construction Corporation, its senior counterpart institution, Kerala State R&B Corporation is an extremely lean organization, concentrating on the financial essentials of projects. Operation and maintenance of the eight National Highways, that pass through the state are under the charge of the National Highway Department that is supervised by the National Highway Authority of India from Delhi.

The network of state and district highways as well as panchayat and municipal roads, more than 130, 000 KM long, is under the charge of state PWD. By and large, these roads are ill-maintained, poorly managed, and yet to catch up with the modern culture of road signs. Successive ministries gave very little attention to improve the work culture of state PWD, which is looked upon as milch cow by opportunist politicians. In the recent past, when the entire Kerala media and people at large were debating over the need or desirability of widening NH-47 and NH-17, Kerala PWD was conspicuously silent: its views were not even sought after. The situation spoke volumes for the lack of expertise and professionalism in the management of our transport infrastructure.

Loss of capacity to govern and to develop and manage infrastructure is a glaring reality in Kerala: Poorly managed roads and bridges are a common, sight everywhere: There are potholes everywhere. The sight of banyan trees growing on the RCC structures of bridges is depressing. Steel bridges hardly get their regular dose of paints. Steel shutters on spillways are attended to, only when people around make a hue and cry, during monsoon floods. PWD or irrigation departments, who are the custodians of these hydraulic strictures, do not consider preventive maintenance as a professional virtue. They are hardly equipped with the tools, expertise and manpower to take up repair and maintenance of such sophisticated structures on a regular basis. These are then contracted out to foreign consultants or the risky jobs get assigned to petty contractors.

Kerala State Electricity Board owns and operates most of the large dams and reservoirs in the state. They are liberally instrumented for detecting and measuring even minor earth tremors. However, the data generated and recorded by them, over the past decades, are hardly used for studying and evaluating the seismic behaviour of the terrain. KSEB has never cared to build up any expertise of its own, on hydrology or dam engineering. KSEB has been developing as a monopoly organization of electrical engineers, and presently, it has little skill or aspiration for the planning, design, operation and maintenance of power generation systems; hydro, thermal, nuclear or non-conventional.

In recent years, it has been specializing in the import and distribution of electric power unlike in the seventies and eighties, when it had in rapid succession completed and commissioned several hydro-electric power plants. It had to its credit, vast experience in investigation, planning, design, and construction of small and medium sized hydro-electric power plants. However, this experience and expertise could not be consolidated and turned into know-how capital of the organization, thanks to its vastly different business plans after the Silent Valley controversy as well as lopsided HRD policies.

This writer remembers even today, the findings of a detailed appraisal of early nineties, on the HRD policies of State Electricity Board: It was predicted that, if the policy distortions are not corrected and large scale recruitment and training resorted to at various levels, there will be hardly anybody left to manage KSEB, by the turn of the century.

In fact, by the year 2000 even the worse was happening: Vacuum at the top was quite visible, and KSEB was turning more and more dependent on petty contractors and contract workers for the operation and maintenance of its sophisticated equipment and systems.

Management and development of modern grid power systems demand, apart from traditional engineering skills, a fairly high level of exposure to Information and Communication Technologies (ICT). The recent legal exposures, related to the software contract given out to a South Korean firm, have revealed the extremely low level of in-house engineering and ICT capabilities within the KSEB organization.

Situation is little different even with regard to non-power utilities like Kerala State Transport Corporation (KSRTC), Kerala Water Authority (KWA), or the other infrastructure development institutions in the public sector. Like KSEB, KSRTC is also a product of central statutes: Developing an effective public transport network on Kerala roads was its founding objective. With its less than 20 % share in passenger buses operating on Kerala roads, KSRTC is unable to play any regulatory or developmental role in the road transport sector. Situation is qualitatively different in most other states, where State Road Transport Corporations virtually dominate the public transport network: People are far less dependent on personal transport, and roads are far more safe and less demanding on maintenance efforts.

Kerala Water Authority (KWA) tells another story of failures on the professional front. Urban sewerage and drainage were also part of KWA responsibility: It was originally designated as Kerala Water & Waste Water Authority (KW&WWA).

As the name got rationalized into KWA, the organization dropped off its drainage and sewerage responsibilities, which were traditionally looked after by local level governments, with the help of what was called the public health engineering department (PHED), which was later abolished, leaving large gaps in institutional responsibilities, including sold waste disposal, which was left virtually uncared for.

Piped water supply is seen as a luxury even today: as a matter of culture and state policy, water supply projects were built only with the support of foreign aid and charity. KWA was seen as an instrument for borrowing and piping in charity. With all sorts of foreign funded projects like British, Dutch and Japanese water supply schemes, KWA did not have a chance to consolidate its experience and expertise and develop its own management systems and technological standards and practices that are tune with the Kerala realities.

Such fundamental weaknesses related to infrastructure development were noticeable, even as early as in the eighties, at the time of the second Nayanar ministry, when this writer had served Kerala Government as its Secretary for the Bureau of Public Enterprises (BPE). Kerala State Planning Board, which was to play a key role in providing policy inputs, had turned dysfunctional by then, thanks to lack of political vision at the state level and proliferation of centrally sponsored schemes. State Public Sector Undertakings, including the public utilities, intended to serve as the extended arms of Government, were looked down as mere commercial enterprises.

R&D institutions and departments initiated in departments like farming, agriculture, irrigation, PWD and others were neglected. Even the Science and Technology institutions established under the State S&T policy of seventies and dedicated to the study of natural resources of the state were not spared from this wanton neglect. By the time, the third Nayanar ministry assumed power in 1996, situation had further deteriorated under the impact of economic and structural reforms. IAS bureaucracy had further strengthened its strangle hold on state administration and Collector Raj was making a reappearance in the districts, reminiscent of the colonial days.

The acute need for capacity building at every level of governance in the states, was felt even by the reform enthusiasts in Delhi: They had tapped UN resources to launch a capacity building program for states like Kerala. Institute in Management in Government (IMG) was entrusted with a substantive project in 1995, aimed at capacity enhancement, and I had served it as a UNIDO consultant. However, the project was a virtual non-starter: Peoples Planning was the priority agenda for LDF ministry and not capacity building. UDF Government, that came in next, had launched a Modernization in Government Program (MGP) with a massive e-governance component. Instead of genuine capacity building and strengthening of governance, the last LDF government launched its Kudumbasree, which has turned out to be a Frankenstein of sort. It is now being countered by the Jana Sree of UDF.

Possibly, situation is no different in other Indian states, as well. Even in states like Gujarat and Maharashtra, where senior most Chief Engineers and other departmental heads doubled up as secretaries to government, situation has been rapidly deteriorating in recent years, thanks to the economic and structural reforms. Central institutions like Planning Commission, Central Electricity Authority, Central Water

Commission, Railways, Shipping Corporation, Oil and Natural Gas Commission (ONGC), Gas Authority of India (GAIL) etc as well as the numerous other central public sector organizations, were under compulsion to devalue or dilute their federal role and responsibilities as the technology generators of the nation. As a result, the capacity of the Union Republic to govern, at central as well as state levels, has been badly eroded.

Even the London Economist has lamented that, Babus and Netas are now on the driving seat of the republic (See special report on India in the Economist of 5th October). Perhaps, that is a far more accurate assessment of the regime in Kerala than that of Thomas Isaac: He had, a couple of years ago, qualified it as *a regime of the babus, for the babus and by the babus.*

---

*   Article in the Passline October, 2012

APARTMENTS: NEW CULTURE WITH AN ECONOMIC RATIONALE*

A dwelling, without a small piece of land around the house, was unthinkable for Malayalees: It could be a tiny piece of land, even as small as a cent or a cent and a half: It was the smell of raw earth around that was important.

But this life style has been costing the society, dear: Unplanned growth of population centres substantially increases the cost of basic infrastructure and civic amenities. Road density in Kerala is 414 km/100 sqkm and it is far ahead of the national average of 75 km. Road length per lakh population in Kerala is 506 km against the national average of 259 km. Kerala with a population density of more than double the national average has already set aside large land areas for road construction. Economy of the state finds it difficult to maintain these vast quantities of roads, constructed year after year. Higher road length per person is also an indicator of the higher outlays subsumed for power and fuel supplies, water supply, sewerage and drainage as well as other utilities. Urbanisation is inevitable, and it was high time that, some sort of discipline was brought into this anarchic situation.

The apartment culture that is slowly setting in Kerala has, therefore, a definite social and economic rationale and the mushrooming real estate and property development business, undoubtedly, are creating real values. I may quote here the personal example of a close friend and comrade-in-arm Kunju Krishnan: we may refer him as KK for convenience. He was a poor man by any standard and working as a helper in a mechanical workshop near his ancestral home, frequently used as a shelter by senior leaders of the left movement, during the dark years of head-hunt by a blood-thirsty police. KK along with his wife and three children was holed up in a small tiled hut, along with his aged ailing mother, when I came across him in the early eighties. He was a known political leader in the locality, sincere to the core, and as usual rewarded less and respected more for his stubborn honesty.

On dividing the family assets, bulk of his ancestral property went to his sisters, married and properly settled elsewhere: Title of the 40 cents of land and the small hut, where KK lived was held by his ailing mother, who was under pressure to divide it once again as family property. He, however, was lucky on the legal front, after the mother died and within no time, property developers closed in on him. For the prices prevailing during late eighties, he got a good bargain: With the cash compensation received for the land, KK could purchase an acre of agricultural land in nearby village, where he built a small farm-house, the two daughters were comfortably married off, and son got educated to work as an accountant in a respectable firm. In addition he was allotted three apartments: As on now, he lives in one and the others are rented out. KK was overnight catapulted into an altogether different social orbit.

More interesting part of this story of large value addition was the bankruptcy of KK's builder, even before the apartments were completed and handed over. The hard liquidity problem of the early nineties, that brought to a complete halt the booming property business, had forced the builder to flee the country. Fortunately for KK, there were enough number of apartment aspirants who had fully paid up for the apartments and ready to go for legal remedies. KK as a man of public interest assembled the necessary expertise, legal, financial as well as technical, to form a cooperative enterprise for raising the balance money and completing the building project. True, he could move into the new flat only four years behind the schedule: However, as per the contract entitlements with the builder, KK continued to stay in his good old place, from where he managed to marry off his two daughters. Despite all odds, he conducted the house warming ceremonies in grand style in the new flat in 1995. Possibly KK's example was more of an exemption: several among the martyrs of the building industry of nineties are yet to recover and a good many among those who invested for apartments continue to wait indefinitely. Moral of the story is obvious: KK and others helped themselves using their collective endeavour.

Belonging to the collective of some eighty and odd apartment dwellers bring in several advantages and privileges. Managing electricity, phone, gas, water, drainage, sewerage and waste disposal collectively is of great advantage. Most apartment collectives have developed their own arrangements for paying up the utility bills and some are offering even internet connections. Convenience shops, common washing and ironing centres are developing as common amenities. A well-kept small garden and children's playground are real luxuries even for the middle class. Instant geriatric care of the old, first aid and emergency medical help are within the reach of the collectives of apartment dwellers. Cultural evenings and festival celebrations are bringing people together in many apartments that simply strengthen our age old secular traditions. Common garages, car parking and 24 hour security at the gate are the new civic amenities that are now taken for granted by every apartment dweller: However these were simply the privileges of the elite classes till yesterday!

The new culture that is developing around our apartments is sure to stay: it is not a passing fad, an apartment, sure, has big cost advantages. However, they are sure to face several serious problems, thanks to their unplanned and totally unregulated growth. Servicing the apartments with infrastructure is posing serious problems: These are to be pre-empted with the help of careful town and country planning, at intra-city as well as intercity levels. Mushrooming of apartments in almost all cities and major towns is sure to discipline Malayalees: They will be forced to redesign the population centres in a far more rational way, consistent with the unique features of the land and water resources.

Kerala, as we know, is a narrow strip of land with a 560 Kilometre coastline on the West, and mountain relief on the East. Every 14 kilometre on the average, there is a river flowing Westward, and forty-one drainage basins rush their heavy monsoon run-off, into a huge inland water body, stretching along the coastline and shaking hands with the Arabian sea, at half a dozen locations called *pozhi*.

Thanks to this unique hydrology, more than half of Kerala population live on its coastal planes, measuring only a third of total land area. This coastal plane, on the two sides of the backwater-network, with its lakes, canals and estuaries, numerous seaports of antiquity and large population centres on either side, is developing into a single modern metro of some twenty million people; population densities crossing the level of 3000 persons per sqkm, for several long stretches.

The North-South inland waterway along this backwater system, and the navigable stretches upstream of the forty-one rivers, were developed by several generations of Kerala rulers, before and after the great Cheraman Perumal who took to Islam. This 1700 Kilometre long inland waterway network was the backbone of Kerala economy and served the culture and commerce of the region for centuries. Due to a variety of factors, neglect and ignorance in the main, these arteries of history turned dysfunctional, within a few decades of Indian independence, inflicting heavy damages on Kerala economy and culture.

These are the unique features of Kerala that had encouraged Abdul Kalam, former President of India, to recommend the development of what he described as smart waterways. Possibly, not only water supply and drainage systems but also power, fuel, communication and transportation systems are to be part of the smart water ways he was dreaming of. Reconstruction of the economy and culture of Kerala along its ancient waterways, with the help of modern Science and Technology, could be the twenty-first century dream project of a **Socialist** Kerala: Why not re-design our population centres with the help of a master plan for the 560 KM long metro that is emerging along Kerala coast, and using apartments as building blocks?

---

*   Slightly modified version of a Passline article published in November 2007

BENYAMIN: THE UNTOLD STORY*

Benyamin, a Kerala Project Engineer working in Middle East, for the past two decades, has endeared himself to the Non Resident Indians, through his dozen or so short stories and a couple of novels in Malayalam. His novel titled, **Aatujeevitham** (Goat-life or Living like goat), first published in August 2008, has simply stormed the NRI community in the Gulf region.

Benyamin has re-told the storey of Najeeb, an immigrant NRK worker, who had flown into Riyadh, capital city of the Kingdom of Saudi Arabia (KGS) in 1992. He recalls that, the regional economy had just kick-started by then, after the first invasion of Iraq, with USA on the lead. Benyamin himself had landed in the city state of Behrens, as an immigrant technician, on the same day when Najeeb flew into Riyadh: He had met Najeeb and listened to his fifty months long adventures in KSA, several years later.

Najeeb and his fellow-traveller, Hakkim, had left Mumbai and landed in Riyadh international airport, supported by perfectly legal documents as Indian citizens, with work permits and legitimate KSA visas for working in a particular construction company. However, representatives of their employer company did not turn up at the airport to pick them up, as promised by the recruitment agent in Mumbai.

They were cleared by the emigration officials in the early hours of Thursday 9th April 1992 and waited for their sponsors in the lounges of Riyadh airport, until late evening. They were, then, unlawfully picked up and transported across desert lands to far-off animal farms, operated by Arab landlords.

These were large isolated desert farms, set up for the rearing of sheep, goats and camels, within barbed wire enclosures or fencing. These are supposed to be the modern KSA farms. Unlike the traditional Arab ones, they follow business models that need only very few hands to operate: One or two captive immigrant farm hands per farm and an Arab supervisor for a cluster of three or four farms, safely separated by fairly large patches of desert. These farms are located far off from commercial centres that take away the raw farm products such as milk, wool and slaughter animals. In turn, farms are supplied with animal fodder, water and cooked food for the sustenance of farm hands. The business model inevitably provides for in-house mini trucks, for goods transportation.

Immigrants, who are in direct charge of the animals in such pseudo modern farms of KSA, have an animal-like existence. They get on the job training in the tending goats, sheep and camels, as they begin to live among them, right from day one of their capture in modern air terminals or labour camps that double up as informal labour markets. They work 24 hours a day, seven days a week with no monthly or annual breaks: There is no chance, whatsoever, for meeting anybody other than their own Arab supervisors, who were expert task masters equipped with powerful guns and equally intimidating binoculars. Communicating with anybody else in any manner under such isolated desert environment was simply impossible.

Najeeb and Hakkim were living and working in the same neighbourhood for more than four years. They met occasionally by chance or by design and debated on their fate. Otherwise, they were two totally lost souls left to themselves, and communicating with their own personal gods. It was mere chance that they could elope, guided by a well built Turk, Ibrahim Kadiri. In the desert, Hakkim succumbed to dehydration, and after a week long adventure, Najeeb was rescued by an Arab motorist, and then taken care of by Kunjikka, an NRK teashop owner. He was finally deported back to India by KSA police and Indian embassy as the member of an eighty strong team of NRI immigrants.

Such deportations of NRI immigrants from KSA, possibly, are a routine affair: Benyamin tells the Najeeb story through 220 printed pages, with very little of drama or suspense. But, in every one of these printed pages, are reflected the mental and physical torture, as well as the pain of cultural and spiritual deprivation of lower class third world immigrants, who are forced to leave their native countries in search of livelihood. In that sense, every page of this book is an indictment of the callousness and failure of State machinery of the Kingdom of Saudi Arabia as well as that of the Republic of India.

Najeeb and Hakkim had travelled to KSA with valid travel documents of international standards. These Indian citizens were not orphans: they had their friends, comrades and close relatives, who would have, surely, apprehended the local government and registered police complaints on loss of contact. KSA is not a lawless country, not to take follow up action on such serious complaints, unless some body influential in local government had a stake or vested interests. Nothing happens on these lines, in the story as told by the novel: Benyamin is silent on such acts of omissions and commissions, criminal neglect or irrational behaviour on the part of authorities in KSA as well as or India. He seems to accept the disappearance of Najeeb and Hakkim as something perfectly normal and natural.

Maybe, such criminal neglect or irrational behaviour by the state machinery on both sides of the migration border is a reality or common life experience of the vast majority of low-skilled Indian workers that migrate to KSA, Kuwait and several other countries of the region. Work permits and Visas are generally organised and exchanged by private recruitment agencies. Regulation and overview by official bodies are minimal, grossly inefficient and even open to corrupt practices in India as well as in Middle East countries.

In Middle East, recruitment agencies collect the low-skilled immigrant workers at the airport: They are then parked in lodgings and forced to surrender passports and other travel documents. The agents act as arbitrators for finding a suitable employer for the new arrivals, and also for fixing the terms and conditions of engagement. This by itself is illegal because an immigrant is not supposed to enter these countries, without a perfectly valid work permit or visa. Thus, an immigrant worker in a Gulf country is forced to break the laws of the land on the very first day of his perfectly legal arrival. Heroes or anti-heroes of Benyamin could not have been an exemption to this general practice.

Around ten percent of Keralites work or stay outside India, and the bulk of them are in Middle East. Immigrant workers from Kerala, had played a key role in building up the petrodollar economies of most Gulf countries. Their remittances have helped their families to lead a slightly better life than the others. But the heavens they built on foreign soil with their blood and sweat were certainly not theirs, and the net benefits they accrue are hardly commensurate with the inevitable pains and sacrifices that are extracted in the bargain.

Those who rule the country eulogise these immigrant workers as part of a great Indian Diaspora and look at their remittances only as a foreign exchange resource for promoting their own pet selfish schemes. Indian embassies in Gulf countries hardly treat them as citizens to be cared for. Najeebs and Hakkims are hunted down as criminals and extradited back to India in large numbers.

During the current season, more than 5600 Keralites have returned from KSA till May end, thanks to the new immigration practices. Soon, this number will be around 15,000 and by end of June and 35,000 or even 80,000 by the yearend. There are reports of wide spread harassment of immigrant workers in Kuwait: Even workers with valid work permits are being arrested or jailed for questioning and even directly sent to deportation camps. There are complaints that embassy officials hardly intervene in the interest NRI citizens.

The Benyamin story has proved to be an instant hit among NRK emigrants in Middle East, because it was their own story written in their own language and idiom, a story of gross neglect by their own country and Government and then a story of crude exploitation by their employers in foreign land.

The book has crossed fifty editions, within the short span of three years, a record in Indian language publication. Editions in other Indian languages are reportedly on the way and Penguin has already brought out one in English.

---

*   Published in June, 2013 in the Passline.